ALSO AVAILABLE FROM HANS BEUMER:

THE ULTIMATE HAPPINESS SERIES:

TRAVEL GUIDE TO SELF-ACTUALIZATION

THE GLOBAL TRAVELLER SERIES:

20,000 KM BY TRAIN

Visit www.hansbeumer.com

THE GLOBAL TRAVELLER SERIES

KUMANO KODO

The first and only detailed and comprehensive English travel guide for 200 kilometers of thousand-year-old mountainous pilgrimage trails in the heart of the Japanese Kii Mountains, covering two UNESCO World Heritage Pilgrimage Routes: Nakahechi Route and Kohechi Route.

by Hans Beumer

Hans Beumer Publications
2016

Hans Beumer Publications
Feldpark 29
6300 Zug
Switzerland

First edition published in May 2016. This book is available as:
-US Trade Paperback (Color): ISBN 978-3-906861-08-1
-US Trade Paperback (B/W): ISBN 978-3-906861-03-6
-EBook: ISBN 978-3-906861-07-4

Typeset body text in Garamond 11.5
Printed and distributed by Lulu Press, Inc.

www.hansbeumer.com

Pilgrimage
Moves
Body
And
Soul

*A sincere thanks to Audrey
for supporting my Pilgrimage in Solitude.*

TABLE OF CONTENTS

FOREWORD

What motivates a person to walk 200 kilometers over isolated mountainous trails and undergo the hardship of the physical strain and the emotional solitude?

A thousand years ago, the pilgrim on the Kumano Kodo trail would have answered as follows:

"To undergo the suffering and hardship of the long and dangerous trails, combined with frequent cold water purification, is to be relieved from all sins, so that he can receive rebirth and rejuvenation from the Kumano deities living in the Kumano Grand Shrines."

What is your answer?

Read this guide book, take in all the cultural experiences and historical background, the descriptions of the trails and the sights of the Nakahechi and Kohechi Routes from the written words and photos, and then plan to find the answer yourself.

Go to the Kii Mountains in Japan and experience the Kumano Kodo first hand.

Find your own answer to the above question.

This book is part of 'The Global Traveler Series'. Books published under this Series describe the experiences of special and extraordinary travels all over the world. The Series has the intention of helping you advance with your own travel planning, experiences and enjoyment.

drs. Hans Beumer
Global Traveller
May 2016

20 TIPS FOR THE PILGRIM

This travel guide contains 20 useful tips for making your pilgrimage along the Nakahechi and Kohechi Routes of the Kumano Kodo a special and successful experience.

Chapter 5

Tip # 1: *Pilgrim the Kumano Kodo in early Spring time when humidity and rain fall are at their lowest, and you can admire the cherry blossoms dotting the landscapes.*

Chapter 6, Section 1

Tip # 2: *Use the stamp list from the Pilgrimage center as checklist for the locations where you should find stamps.*

Tip # 3: *Book your stay at one of the hotels with a hot spring, at one of the Onsen (Kawayu Onsen, Yunomine Onsen or Wataze Onsen), and enjoy a muscle relaxant hot spring bath after a strenuous hiking day.*

Tip # 4: *Arrange your meal requirements for the next day before 7 p.m.*

Chapter 6, Section 5

Tip # 5: *The wind on the river can be cold, so depending on the time of year, bring a jacket or sweater.*

Tip # 6: *When at the Tourist Information Center in Hongu Taisha, and you have already visited the Kamikura-jinja Shrine, or you intend to visit this Shrine, have them put stamp number 34 in your booklet.*

Chapter 6, Section 7

Tip # 7: When visiting Nachi Taisha, stay at a Ryokan in Kii Katsuura, where you can enjoy the Onsen hot spring baths.

Chapter 6, Section 8

Tip # 8: Depending on the time of year of your hike, the wind, coming from the Ocean through the main valley, can be cold. So bring a warm jacket or sweater.

Tip # 9: Plan your arrival in Koguchi in such a way that you have a good chance of catching the public bus, without having to wait for hours. Sort out the bus time tables in advance, either via the Internet or at the local Tourist Information Center. In case you want to spend the night at one of the three accommodations in the village, make sure that you make your reservation well in advance.

Chapter 6, Section 9

Tip # 10: Consider booking your accommodation in one of the Onsen close by (Kawayu, Wataze or Yunomine), so that you can relax in a hot spring bath after completing your day hike.

Chapter 7

Tip # 11: In case you are not close to Koyasan, sort out your train or bus time tables. HyperDia (www.Hyperdia.com) is good for planning your train trip, costs and times. You might have to allocate a day to get to Koyasan.

Tip # 12: Visit the Tourist Office in Koyasan to obtain your first stamp, the special Kohechi stamp booklet and local sightseeing brochures.

Tip # 13: Plan to have at least a full day of sightseeing in Koyasan, as there are many interesting Buddhist buildings and historical places to experience.

Tip # 14: Plan your visit to Koyasan in Spring time, ideally April or May.

Tip # 15: Get up early to attend the Buddhist morning prayer and meditation session from 6 till 7:30 a.m.

Chapter 7, Section 1

Tip # 16: Carry four stamp booklets to collect all your stamps when hiking the Nakahechi and the Kohechi Routes.

Chapter 7, Section 2

Tip # 17: Book your stays along the Kohechi Route long in advance. This is easily done via the Kumano Travel Office (www.kumano-travel.com) Community Reservation System.

Tip # 18: You are hiking through remote and isolated mountain areas. During most of the Kohechi trail there is cellphone reception, so make sure that you carry a cellphone for emergency cases, particularly when you are travelling alone. Have the local emergency numbers pre-programmed.

Chapter 7, Section 4

Tip # 19: Come prepared with rain gear. In case you have flexibility in your day planning you could also sit out a half day or day of rain.

Tip # 20: Carry a walking cane or hiking sticks, not only for providing support during ascents and descents, but also to fend off any snakes or other animals on the pathway.

Chapter 1

THE 1'000 YEARS OLD PILGRIMAGE

History of Kumano Kodo

Kumano is the old name of the mountainous and isolated rain forested region at the heart and lower half of the Kii Peninsula in Japan. Literally translated from the Kanji characters, Kumano means "Bear Field" also called "Barbarian Area" or "Refuge Area". In ancient times (8th century) when Nara used to be the capital of Japan, the mountainous lands South of the capital were considered to be largely impregnable and an area for the non-educated and non-sophisticated local people. During ancient times of war, the people from Nara would flee to the South and seek refuge in those mountains. Up to some 200 years ago, the Kumano region had a culture of its own, with only very few rice fields, where the local population lived from hunting deer or fishing in the rivers. It was a very poor area. About 120 years ago, the name Kumano for the region disappeared, as the area was split up between the Prefectures of Nara, Mie and Wakayama.

Kodo means old route or pilgrimage.

Kumano Kodo is the collective name for six pilgrimage routes to the three Kumano Grand Shrines, also called the Sanzan, located in the Southeastern part of the Kii Peninsula. Pilgrimage to the **Kumano Sanzan** Shrines started in the 10th century and experienced its highlight during the following four centuries. Because royalties and dignitaries travelled with a large entourage of up to 800 people in total, and the mountain trails were narrow, they had to walk in a procession of long lines, so it was also described as "a pilgrimage of ants to Kumano".

Kumano Kodo is about suffering, making the pilgrim clear his sins. The suffering is caused by the hardship experienced during the trekking through the difficult mountainous region. The pilgrims used to purify themselves by washing in the cold mountain streams along the perilous path. The combination of suffering and purification gave its meaning to the Kumano Kodo. Upon arrival at the three Grand Shrines, the pilgrims would revitalize themselves and all their sins would have been cleared.

You need to consider that more than a thousand years ago the means of transportation were limited to flat bottom river barges, horseback, walking, and for the emperor and other dignitaries, to be carried by servants. There were no roads and it was a dangerous journey to undertake in those days. Getting to the Kumano Sanzan from Kyoto would take one month and would have been very dangerous, with difficulties of finding food, shelter and risks of losing the way. In order to help the pilgrims on their way, many Oji, used for prayers and direction, were placed along the route, and commercial people set up tea-houses for rest and refreshments for the pilgrims. Information travelled slow in those days, thus the meeting points of the tea-houses were important for exchanging information amongst the travelers, particularly between those coming and going. The royalties and dignitaries probably did not have that much hardship during their pilgrimage to the Kumano Sanzan, as they were being carried or pulled on river barges, and had a large entourage of servants (between 200 and 800) taking care of their physical needs and wellbeing. For a pilgrim travelling alone or in the company of just another person, however, this must have been quite different. A perilous trip into unknown mountainous areas, often under difficult weather conditions, with simple clothing and limited food supplies. You can imagine that this was severe hardship, and enduring this hardship and suffering was an important part of the pilgrimage. Hence the many Oji along the trail, providing opportunities for prayers for safety and spiritual comfort to complete the journey to reach the Grand Shrines at Hongu Taisha, Hayatama Taisha and Nachi Taisha.

Nowadays pilgrims and tourists hiking the old trails have it very easy compared to thousand years ago. The focus of today's pilgrim is mostly on traversing the ancient trails, enjoying the old pathways through dense and isolated forests, admiring the Temples, Shrines and Oji, but still enduring some of the hardship and suffering as a number of these trails are still exhausting for the modern day hiker. The silence of the forests combined with the spirituality of the pathways, through the passing of many Shrines and Oji, make this, even today, a very special experience. Arriving at one of the three Grand Shrines is still a milestone in the life of the modern day Kumano Kodo hiker and pilgrim, as you will be in awe from the symbolisms and spirituality of the place, as well as the feeling of obtaining your reward for the suffering during the several days of hiking. That is of course when one pilgrims the whole route the old fashioned way, and doesn't take any short cuts by using a tourist sightseeing coach, bus or car.

UNESCO World Heritage

In 2004, Kumano Kodo was registered under the UNESCO World Heritage, as "Sacred Sites and Pilgrimage Routes in the Kii Mountain Range, and the cultural landscapes that surround them". There are three main aspects to the Kumano Kodo:

1. *The sacred sites of Koyasan, Kumano Sanzan, and Yoshino and Omine.* These sites have been declared as a World Heritage site, and for good reasons. In this book you find elaborate descriptions and photos relating to Koyasan (Chapter 7) and the Kumano Sanzan (Chapter 6).

2. *The ancient pilgrim routes that connect these sacred sites to the former capital cities of Nara and Kyoto.* The journey itself over perilous mountain trails to the sacred sites was an important element for the religious experience. The Kumano Kodo Routes registered under the UNESCO World Heritage are the Nakahechi Route, the Kohechi Route and the Omine Okugakemichi Route, with a total length of around 308 kilometers. In the remainder of this book you will find elaborate descriptions of the ancient Nakahechi (Chapter 6) and Kohechi (Chapter 7) Routes, accompanied by many photos, visualizing my experiences.

3. *The dense forests and landscapes of the Kii Mountains, with its many streams, rivers and waterfalls.* The natural environment of dense rain forests, with only very few roads and access points, provides an extraordinary hiking experience. On certain sections of the Routes, you can walk for hours without meeting a single soul. Along the way there are panoramic viewpoints on the mountain ranges and on crystal clear rivers snaking through the valleys and in Nachi Taisha you find Japan's highest waterfall. In the next chapters of this book you will find a multitude of photos revealing these reasons for inclusion to the World Heritage.

According to UNESCO, one of the main contributors to the heritage of the Kumano Kodo is the fact that its traditions and sites have been extraordinary well-documented and maintained over a period of more than 1'200 years. I can confirm that when visiting the Kumano Sanzan, Koyasan and the many Temples and Shrines, and seeing the Oji, Jizo and Kannon along the isolated trails, you indeed feel teleported a thousand years back in time.

The Kii Peninsula

The Kumano region lies in the heart and lower half of the Kii Peninsula, which in its turn lies South of the main cities of Osaka, Kyoto and Nara. Kii Tanabe is often regarded as the gateway to the Kumano Kodo and is about 150 kilometers South of Osaka, 200 kilometers South of Kyoto, and 165 kilometers South of Nara. Forested mountains with elevations between 600 and 2'000 meters make up the greater part of the inlands of the peninsula. There are a number of roads that follow the rivers in the valleys, and a few roads cut through the mountains. Railway lines are only along the coast line. Most small villages in the valleys are only accessible by one road, and although there is quite an extensive bus network, the frequency of the buses is relatively low and seasonally dependent, accounting for the long duration it takes to get from one valley to another.

The weather conditions on the Kii Peninsula can make the pilgrimage quite challenging. Typhoons (hurricanes) regularly hit the Kii Peninsula, bringing strong winds and enormous amounts of precipitation in the period between May and October, most heavily during August and September. Most of the Kii Peninsula is covered by dense rainforest with high levels of humidity caused by the high levels of rainfall during the summer months.

The sparse population on the peninsula traditionally lived from forestry in the inland and fishing along the coast line. The population is declining, and many young people moved to the big cities, leaving mostly the elderly behind. The tourist sector, driven by the Kumano Kodo, is one of the most important generators of income for the local population, through the offering of accommodations and travel organizations.

Chapter 2

THE 6 KUMANO KODO ROUTES

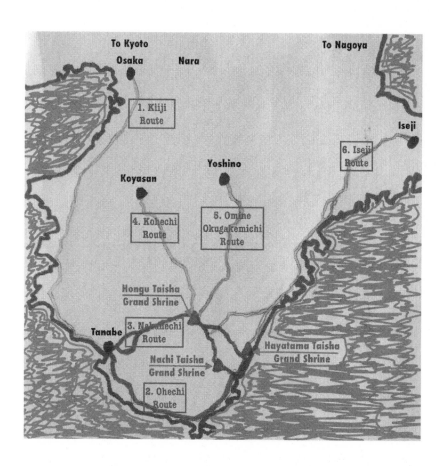

The Kumano Kodo consists of six pilgrimage routes:
1. Kiiji Route
2. Ohechi Route
3. Nakahechi Route
4. Kohechi Route
5. Omine Okugakemichi Route
6. Iseji Route

1.Kiiji Route

In ancient times, the Kiiji Route was the starting point of the Kumano Kodo. The Kiiji Route starts in Kyoto and finishes in Kii-Tanabe. It has a length of about 200 kilometers and broadly follows the present main road and railway line along the West coast of the Kii Peninsula. When this pilgrimage practice started a 1'000 years ago, this route might have been well traversed. At that time Kyoto was the capital of Japan, and logical starting point for many pilgrims. From Kyoto to Osaka the emperor and his family would probably have travelled by boat on the Yodogawa River, and from Osaka to Kii Tanabe on horseback, being carried or walking. Simple peasants and servants would of course walk the whole route.

Nowadays the route from Kyoto to Kii Tanabe can be easily travelled by car, taking only two hours to cover the 200 kilometers. Starting from Wakayama city, for about 80 of the 200 kilometers, hiking route maps are available in Japanese. The 80 and 200 kilometers distances are measured when travelling on the road. The Kumano Kodo hiking trail from Wakayama to Kii Tanabe, however, according to the Japanese trail maps, measures around 136 kilometers (instead of the 80 kilometers by road), which would take an estimated 7 days to complete.

The Kiiji Route is not listed under the UNESCO World Heritage Pilgrimage Routes.

The Kiiji Route connects seamless to the Ohechi and Nakahechi Routes. The Ohechi Route starts in Kii-Tanabe and continues to follow the coast, along the South point of the Kii Peninsula. The Nakahechi Route starts in Kii-Tanabe and goes inland into the Kii Mountain range.

2.Ohechi Route

The Ohechi Route starts in Kii-Tanabe and continues to follow the West coast to the South point of the Kii Peninsula and then North along the East coast to Nachi. It has a length of about 100 kilometers and broadly follows the present main road and railway line along the South coast of the Peninsula. It is the coastal road to the Kumano Sanzan region and was mostly used from the 16th century, offering great views on the beaches and Ocean.

The local Tourist Office could only provide a route map in Japanese. Presumable not many pilgrims walk this route, which would take an estimated 5 days to complete, though the trail maps cover only about 70% of the complete route.

The Ohechi Route is not listed under the UNESCO World Heritage Pilgrimage Routes.

3.Nakahechi Route

The Nakahechi Route is the most popular route of the Kumano Kodo, attracting the most tourists and pilgrims. This route is made famous by the pilgrimage scenes photographed in Nachi Taisha, which feature in many of the brochures for Kumano Kodo.

The present day Nakahechi Route usually has its starting point at the Takijiri-Oji (Wakayama Prefecture), which is 40 minutes by bus from Kii Tanabe (from the West), or one hour and 25 minutes by bus from Hongu Taisha (from the East). Takijiri-Oji is an isolated place in a valley in the mountains, without accommodations, so must be reached by bus or other means of transportation to start your hike.

The Nakahechi Route covers a distance of about 90 kilometers (including ca. 16 kilometers over the Kumano-gawa River) till you arrive at Nachi Taisha.

From Nachi Taisha the pilgrims used a 'shortcut' to get back to Hongu Taisha, and from there on used the same trail back to Tanabe and Kyoto. When you add-in this 'shortcut' to get back to Hongu Taisha, the total length of the Nakahechi trail increases to ca. 118 kilometers (including ca. 16 kilometers over the Kumano-gawa River).

Finally, when you add the additional route from Hongu Taisha to Yunomine Onsen as described in Chapter 6, section 3 and the Section 4 (chapter 6) 'shortcut' to Yunomine Onsen, you end up with a total trail length of ca. 128 kilometers (including ca. 16 kilometers over the Kumano-gawa River).

The trails take you over several mountain passes, generally ranging between 300 and 600 meters in altitude, with the exception of two passes along the Ogumotori-goe section, which take you to a level of almost 900 meters.

There are good and detailed route maps for all sections, but for sections 6 and 7 (see Chapter 6) they are only in Japanese. All route maps can be obtained at the Kumano Tourist Offices or online at www.tb-kumano.jp. Accommodations along the route can be easily booked via the Kumano Travel Reservation System (www.kumano-travel.com).

Chapter 6 covers the Nakahechi Route in detailed descriptions, with the support of many photos, so please find out more details there. In that Chapter you will read how the traditional Nakahechi Route extends beyond the present day popular four days/sections of the hiking trails.

For those pilgrims that want to start their walk in Kii Tanabe, only Japanese language route maps are available (handed out by the Tourist Information Office). The trail from Kii Tanabe station to Takijiri-oji has a length of about 17 kilometers.

The Nakahechi Route is listed under the UNESCO World Heritage Pilgrimage Routes.

4.Kohechi Route

The Kohechi Route starts in Koyasan and finishes in Hongu Taisha, with a length of ca. 73 kilometers. This route provides a direct access from the area North of Koyasan, such as Nara, to the Kumano Sanzan region, and was a most frequently traversed pilgrimage route until the 17th century.

Koyasan (Nara Prefecture) is a small town which consist mostly of Temples and Shukubo (Temple-Inns). The Temples focus on Buddhist practices and studies, following the Shingon Buddhism. Koyasan was founded in the year 816 by a Buddhist monk called Kobo Daishi, who wanted to have a Buddhist retreat deep in the mountains. For more than a thousand years, people have undertaken a pilgrimage to Koyasan to experience this small and isolated Buddhist mountain retreat.

The mountain town, at an elevation of around 900 meters, is an excellent starting point for the Kohechi Route. The Kohechi Route trails take you over four mountain passes, ranging between 1'000 and 1'250 meters in altitude. There are good and detailed route maps for the four days of this hike, which can be obtained at the Kumano Tourist Offices or online at www.tb-kumano.jp. Accommodations along the route can be easily booked via the Kumano Travel Reservation System (www.kumano-travel.com).

Chapter 7 covers the Kohechi Route with detailed descriptions supported by many photos, so please find out more details there.

This route is listed under the UNESCO World Heritage Pilgrimage Routes.

5. Omine Okugakemichi Route

The Omine Okugakemichi Route starts in Yoshino (Nara Prefecture) and finishes in Hongu Taisha, with a length of over 90 kilometers. It is called the Mountainous Route because 80% of the route is at elevations between 1'000 and 2,000 meters above sea-level, and crosses seven mountain passes above 1'700 meters in altitude.

For the Omine Okugakemichi Route, only Japanese language route maps are available, and these route maps have a very limited level of detail. It is a dangerous remote route, away from villages and service points, taking 7 to 10 days to complete. This route is hardly traversed by tourists and only used as a training for ascetic Buddhist monks, as it involves rock climbing on some parts of the route. The nights will have to be spent camping at cottages and temples, and the trail should only be undertaken after coordination with the temple-monks in Yoshino. They have their contact network with the cottages and shrines along the way, and can ensure availability and access to these accommodations. A guide from Yoshino will be required because of the remoteness, limited signposts and markers, as well as the logistical challenges of carrying sufficient liters of water and dry food, and the contacts (language) to the locals at the accommodations.

In case you understand the Japanese language, you can visit the following website to try to find out more information: www.vill.totsukawa.lg.jp.

This route is listed under the UNESCO World Heritage Pilgrimage Routes.

6.Iseji Route

The Iseji Route starts in Ise, a small town in the Mie Prefecture on the North-East side of the Kii Peninsula, and is the Eastern Route to Kumano. This route is the shortest way from the area of Nagoya to the region of the Kumano Sanzan, and was increasingly used from the 17th century. It connects the Ise-jingu Grand Shrine to the area of the three Kumano Grand Shrines.

The route has a length of around 200 kilometers to reach the Hongu Taisha Grand Shrine, which can be done in around 10 days. For most of the time, this route closely follows the JR Kisei Railway line, as well as road number 42. The first ca. 80 kilometers are through mountainous areas, whereas the subsequent ca. 80 kilometers are close to the coast line, and the final ca. 40 kilometers are through the forested mountains. The trail has little elevation, going over passes between 100 and 300 meters in altitude.

Good detailed hiking route maps are available in English and can be obtained at the Tourist Information Offices, or online at the website of www.kumanoco.net.

The Iseji Route is not listed under the UNESCO World Heritage Pilgrimage Routes.

Getting to the Kii Mountains

There are many ways to get to the Kii Peninsula. When travelling from outside Japan, it is easiest to fly directly into Kansai International Airport (KIX). The airport is on an artificial island in Osaka Bay and has easy and frequent train connections to all major cities in the area, such as Osaka, Kyoto and Nara. From the airport it takes about two and a half hours, two trains with one transfer, to get to Kii Tanabe, the Kumano Kodo entrance point. It takes that long not because of the large distance, but because the train tracks closely follow the coast line with its many bends and tunnels. The price of a ticket (on the express train) from Kansai Airport to Kii Tanabe is 3'890 Yen ($35).

There are frequent trains from Tokyo (5 hours 45 minutes), Kyoto (3 hours 30 minutes), Nara (3 hours 30 minutes) and Osaka (3 hours) to Kii Tanabe.

Call # 1: There are six Kumano Kodo Routes, but only three of them have route maps and train details in the English language. For the Sections 6 and 7 of the Nakahechi Route, only Japanese language trails maps are available as well. The Tourist Offices of the related Prefectures should consider making these route maps available in English as well.

Chapter 3

THE LOCAL TRAVEL EXPERIENCES

The Japanese culture differs quite a bit from the Western and other Asian cultures. Within the general Japanese culture, the common practices and local habits in the heart of the Kii Mountains on the Kii peninsula seem to bestow an extra dimension to this culture. The purpose of Chapters 3, 4 and 5 is to elaborate on those local cultural aspects in order to manage your expectations for what you can encounter during your hiking or pilgrimage on the Kumano Kodo.

Accommodations

During your stay in the Kii Mountains you are likely to come across the following accommodations: regular business hotel, Ryokan, Minshuku and Shukubo. Most of these accommodations can be easily booked through the Kumano Travel Community Reservation System (www.kumano-travel.com), however, requiring full prepayment. Make sure that you bring those printed accommodation vouchers with you, just in case you need to show them at your check-in, although most of the time your passport is sufficient to identify your booking. Some of the accommodations do not have a presence on English language hotel booking websites, so unless you can read Japanese websites, you will be limited to the Kumano Travel Organization for these reservations.

Regular **business hotels** are available in the larger towns, for example in Shingu and Tanabe. They are not available in the small villages or locations in the mountains with the Onsen. The regular business hotel provides good value for money and is usually much lower priced than a Ryokan or Shukubo. In the business hotel you will have a normal bed and an ensuite bathroom with your own toilet, sink and bath/shower. It is what you are used to in the West, for example, you don't need to take off your shoes when entering the building. Generally, a meal plan is not included and they don't provide lunch packets, but their restaurant will have extensive opening times for breakfast and dinner.

During your hike along the Nakahechi Route it is possible to stay at the regular business hotels, for example in Tanabe or Shingu.

Along the Kohechi Route there are no such business hotels.

A **Ryokan** is an accommodation in traditional Japanese style. You have your own room, and the size of the room is measured in the number of tatami mats covering the floor space. In such a room you often have a low table, a floor seat with a cushion, a safe for your valuables, a heater or air-conditioning and a TV, and at the front towards the window a little table with two normal, though low chairs. In the more expensive Ryokans you have a toilet, shower/bath and sink ensuite to your own room. In other Ryokans you might have only a toilet and sink ensuite to your room. The latter is often the case when you are at an Onsen, where the bath and washing facilities are centralized at the hot spring area inside the Ryokan. Meals are served either in your room, or in the Ryokan's restaurant.

The Ryokan provides accommodation, dinner and breakfast as well as a lunch box for the overnight guests, usually in one package price. Ryokans can be relatively expensive but are an excellent way of experiencing the traditional Japanese culture and hospitality. You find more details and descriptions in the next Chapters.

Ryokans are available along the Nakahechi Route and three out of four locations along the Kohechi Route.

Ryokan room

A **Minshuku** is an accommodation where you don't have your own room in the traditional sense, but where the sleeping space for guests is separated by sliding doors. You leave your shoes behind the front door, before you step on the elevated floor with the tatami mats. In such a 'room' you only have a futon, blanket and a basket with your towel and yukata; there are no locks and you don't have a safe for your valuables. The shower and toilet are at the back of the building and have to be shared between all visitors, and with the owners as well. Meals are taken by the visitors together in a separate room. There is little to no privacy as during daytime the sliding doors will be open.

The Minshuku provides accommodation, dinner and breakfast as well as a lunch box for the overnight guests, usually in one package price. A Minshuku is a relatively inexpensive way of organizing your accommodation during your Kumano Kodo. You find more details and descriptions in Chapter 7.

Minshuku type accommodations are available along both the Nakahechi and Kohechi Routes.

Minshuku sleeping space

A **Shukubo** is a Temple-inn run by monks and provides accommodation, dinner and breakfast for the overnight guests. All rooms have tatami mats and sliding doors. The sliding doors have no locks, but the room has a small safe for valuables. The table is low, and there are no chairs, as you sit on a cushion with crossed legs or with your legs under the low table. There is no TV in the room.

Most tourists travel in groups and share a large room per group. That means that in one room multiple futon mats are placed next to each other, each covered with a thick blanket against the cold. Each room does have a heater, and the low table has an electrically heated blanket underneath, with which to cover your folded legs. All shoes are left in a rack outside, at the entrance of the building. You get to wear the one-size-fit-all slippers for all indoor walkways. The slippers are left outside the rooms in the hallway; you don't wear them in your room.

Dinner and breakfast are typically served in the room for the larger groups, whereas for individuals or couples, dinner is served in the room, but breakfast in a common room. The meals are Buddhist vegetarian, called Shojin Ryori, and include a soup dish, a grilled dish, a pickled dish, a deep fried dish, and a tofu dish. They don't provide lunch packages for your hiking day. The rooms have no toilet, sink or bath; these facilities are separate, and shared between all the guests.

The overnight price at a Shukubo generally lies in between the price of a Ryokan and a Minshuku. On the Nakahechi Route there are no Shukubo for you to stay in. If you want to stay in a Temple-inn run by monks, you will need to travel to Koyasan, which is the starting point of the Kohechi Route.

The overnight stay at the Shukubo is special, because you can observe and 'participate' in the monks' morning prayers and mediation session. You find more details and descriptions in Chapter 7.

Entrance to Shukubo

Room

Other practical experiences:

At several of the traditional accommodations, the door-opening to the room, as well as the sliding doors in the room, have a height of only 1.75 meter. So when you are taller than that, duck your head when entering.

Often the door to your room does not automatically lock when you pull the door closed. You need to turn the lock with your key in order to lock it.

At the Shukubo in Koyasan, the futon has a length of only 175 centimeters. If you are taller than that, your heels and feet will be on the floor.

Your futon will be made by housekeeping while you are at dinner.

The toilet at your accommodation will be very comfortable. The toilet seat will be heated and you can clean your bottom with an automated warm water spray. But be aware that some of the public toilets along your hiking routes may be the old fashioned squat toilets.

Quite often the traditional accommodations have Wi-Fi only in the lobby. I was in several Ryokans which had no Wi-Fi connection in the room, or where the Wi-Fi access in the room was the Wakayama free Wi-Fi connection, for which a separate registration from the hotel's Wi-Fi in the lobby was necessary. So don't expect seamless access to Wi-Fi in all areas of your accommodation. Surprisingly, at the Temple-inn in Koyasan, the monks had set up a very good Wi-Fi connection, covering all areas, including the guest rooms. At the Minshuku I could only get access to Wi-Fi when I went close towards the front door.

In most of your accommodations you have a TV in your room. But don't get your hopes up for HBO, Cinemax, or any other English language channel for that matter. The number of channels will be limited to nine, and all will be in Japanese.

You will see that most of the household staff is of an elderly age, particularly in the more remote mountainous regions. You won't meet a lot of young people at those locations because of the ageing of the Japanese population, and because young people leave the area to study and work in one of the bigger cities like Wakayama.

Because the summers are hot and humid, most accommodations have an air-conditioning system in the guest rooms, which can be used for cooling as well as heating. Some older and more traditional accommodations may not have that, but at minimum will have a gas heater, which does leave a smell and the burning flames make a sound. I can imagine that such gas heaters are a common cause for fires in those wooden buildings. So be careful.

Inside the traditional accommodations you don't wear your shoes; you leave them at the entrance area in a rack. You will need to wear slippers inside the building, and most slippers are one-size-fit-all, without distinction between male, female or foot size. Because they are made of smooth plastic, you will often lose them, particularly when ascending or descending the stairs. In the toilet area you change slippers: a separate pair of 'toilet slippers' will have to be used in that area. As mentioned before, you don't wear the slippers on tatami mats, meaning that you leave the slippers in front of your room and in front of the restaurant. You also put your slippers in a rack at the entrance of the Onsen hot spring bath. At one Ryokan, staff would neatly arrange all shoes at the entrance area, and even place a room number next to the shoes.

Slippers and shoes (by room nr.) at the Ryokan entrance

Toilet area slippers

In case you are travelling with heavy or bulky luggage, which you don't want to or can't carry during your day hike on the trail, you can make use of the luggage forwarding service. This is a reservation system providing a shuttle service, bringing your luggage from one accommodation to another. It can be booked via the Kumano-Travel service.

Dinner, Breakfast, and Lunch Box

As described above, in most of the accommodations you will have a meal plan, including breakfast, dinner and a lunch box. Dinner, on the evening that you arrive, and breakfast, the next morning before you depart, are traditional Japanese set meals. Usually there is no menu or à-la-carte choice for food. At some of the accommodations you can however chose between Japanese or Western set meal. Chose the Japanese set meal, enabling you to taste and experience the local ingredients, and have a high protein, low carbohydrates meal. The Japanese breakfast and dinner are served with many small portions of different types of food. At dinner you are likely to have a small barbeque or hot pot bowl which is heated and where your meat or small fish is grilled, rice is cooked (sometimes with peas), or soup is boiled.

Your only choice is for drinks like beer, sake, soda or tea. Generally, they don't serve coffee, neither after dinner, nor at breakfast, but there is always an unlimited supply of green tea. Most accommodations that are used to hikers, don't serve lunch in their restaurant. In case you are spending the day at the accommodation, for example because of the heavy rainfall, you will probably need to go outside for lunch, or request the lunch box the evening before.

The meals for the travel group will be served all at once. When you enter the restaurant at the pre-set time of your meal, part of the preset meal will already be on the table. When you travel alone, you get a small table for yourself. Often your name or room number is displayed on a card on the table, or even at the restaurant door, in case the accommodation has multiple rooms where meals are taken.

First course of pre-set dinner

Dinner room with name

At the traditional accommodations like the Ryokans, the meal times are strict. Upon your arrival and check-in, you will have to make a choice at what time you want to have dinner and breakfast. The choice for the dinner time is usually 6, 6:30 or 7 p.m., and for breakfast 7, 7:30 or 8 a.m. The accommodations show relatively little to no flexibility for enabling meals outside these times. If you leave before 7 a.m., you won't be able to get an earlier breakfast. Apparently the cook and service staff do not start very early.

If you want a lunch box for the next day hike, you need to request one before dinner time the previous evening. If you are too late with your request, they won't be able to whip up a lunch box to take away the next morning, because the cook will already have left right after dinner. The lunch box itself contains mostly rice, perhaps with some omelet (tamago) and pickles. Because you will likely carry the lunch box in your backpack, it is good that it only contains dry food. Having a lunch box day after day, however, very quickly becomes monotonous. You have rice for breakfast, for lunch and dinner. At least during breakfast and dinner there are many other small dishes as well, but in your lunch box it is almost only rice balls.

Lunchbox

The guest rooms usually have a refrigerator, but it is almost always empty. You can buy your cold drinks from the vending machine in the lobby of the hotel. You can buy beer, sake, as well as sodas, cold coffee and mineral water, whatever you need in your room or to take away for your day hike.

Vending machines

The Public Bus

Even when you are part of a tour group, it is likely that you will need to take the public bus to get from your accommodation to the starting point of your day hike, and/or from the end point of your day hike back to your accommodation.

Riding the bus is different from what you are used to. You can't buy tickets in advance, and you don't enter at the front of the bus. Instead you enter through the doors in the middle of the bus.

Upon entering you must draw a small ticket from the ticket machine at the right or left side of the entrance. This ticket is a small stub with a number, representing the bus stop number/location where you entered the bus. At the front of the bus, above the windshield, a large electronic table displays the number of each of the bus stops, and below that number the amount of the fare that needs to be paid. For example, if you get on the bus at stop number 11, your ticket number will be 11, and when the bus arrives at bus stop number 12, the amount could be 100 Yen. Upon arriving at bus stop number 13 the amount will increase, for example to 250 Yen, and so forth. My most expensive bus ride cost 1,980 Yen, from Yunomine Onsen to Kii Tanabe station, taking almost two hours. In some buses this electronic display also shows the names of the upcoming bus stop in Japanese and sometimes in English. At the same time the upcoming bus stop names are called over the loudspeaker in Japanese, and sometimes also in English.

When your stop is coming up, push the stop button and when the bus halts, walk to the front of the bus. You can read the exact amount to be paid from the display at the front of the bus. Payment is in cash only, so make sure that you carry enough coins and 1'000 Yen notes. Next to the chauffeur there is a changing machine for coins and 1'000 Yen notes. Just insert the note into the machine, and it will spit out the same amount in coins. You insert your number stub together with the correct amount of coins for your bus fare into the register, which records the amount that you paid. You get no receipt or ticket stub.

The bus drivers speak little to no English, but are extremely friendly and will always assist you in case you have difficulties with this system. When the bus is not so full, the driver may even ask you where you want to go and make a special announcement to you when your stop is coming up. You can always walk up to the bus driver and make the special request that he lets you know when your stop is due.

Bus *Bus stop*

Ticket stub machine and Overhead fare display and fare machine

Cash

Bring sufficient foreign currency cash to change into Yen notes, because you will need it. The small villages in the Kii Mountains have no banks where you can change currency, so it is advisable to change upon arrival at the airport. Some of the bigger towns, like Shingu and Tanabe, have ATMs to withdraw cash, but you would need to coordinate your Yen currency requirements with being at these locations.

When you make (part of) your reservations through the Kumano Travel Community Reservation System, you will have prepaid your overnight stays. Accommodations booked directly via English language hotel booking websites likely need to be paid at the time of check-in or check-out. It can happen that an accommodation does not accept credit cards, but only cash settlement of the bill.

Many of your drinks can be obtained from convenience stores or vending machines (often outside the same convenience store or in the hotel lobby). They mostly operate with cash, coins and 1'000 Yen notes.

All bus fares, as described above, need to be paid in cash.

Access to certain Temples and other tourist activities will usually have to be paid in cash.

Though the amounts are usually small (apart from the accommodation cash payment), they do add up, especially if you are staying longer than just a few days.

Language

Apart from a few exceptions, most local people, and particularly the elderly, don't speak any English. That is no problem at all, and makes the communication process adventurous. At one Ryokan a short old lady served me my breakfast and dinner, and she kept speaking to me in Japanese, even though I could not understand a word. I kept speaking back to her in English with a few Japanese words, but still I think that we understood each other pretty well.

Sometimes, however, you also get lost in translation. On one occasion, the heating was not working in my room, so I called down to the front desk. The first person who answered the phone did not understand my question, so I got connected to three more hotel staff. The fourth staff asked me whether I wanted to know the time of my dinner. I had to go down to the front desk and ask for an English speaking manager in order to get the problem with the room's heating resolved.

There are many Japanese phrase books that you can buy or useful phrases which you can find on the Internet. The following few phrases and greetings are very helpful in establishing a polite relationship with the local people:

Hello	Konnichi Wa
Good morning	Ohayo Gozaimasu
Good evening	Konban Wa
Thank you	Arrigato Gozaimasu
Thank you very much	Domo Arrigato Gozaimasu
Yes	Hai
Please	Dozo
Excuse me	Sumimasen
I don't understand	Wakarimasen
Goodbye	Sayonara

Chapter 4

THE SPIRITUAL AND CULTURAL EXPERIENCES

Temple, Shrine, Oji, Kannon

During your pilgrimage you come across many Temples, Oji, Jizo, Shrines, Kannon and other Buddhist religious buildings and statues. It is good to understand their purpose and meaning.

A **Temple** is a building that houses Buddhist statues, and usually has a name that ends with '–ji'. In front of a temple you will usually find incense burners for purification. Many temples are accompanied by a Pagoda, a multi-tiered tower. The temple is centered around Buddha.

The main Buddha Temple and Pagoda in Koyasan

The main purpose of a **Shrine** is to safeguard the sacred objects contained inside the building, while at the same time providing the housing for the Deities. Many Shrines have features that are unique for Japan, for example the torii archways, of which there can be one or multiple, often painted in the typical orange color. The name of the Shrine is followed by the word '-jingu'.

In front of the Shrines there are troughs filled with fresh water, which are used for purification, cleaning of your hands and mouth before entering. The water comes out of the mouth of a dragon, because the dragon is considered the god of water. Don't swallow the water or touch the large spoons with your mouth tough. In ancient times the pilgrims used to purify themselves in the rivers that they had to cross. The religious procedure at the Shrine is that, after purification, the pilgrims first ring the bell to wake up the deities. Then they toss a small coin (in ancient times rice or vegetables) in the big wooden chest, which is to pay for the wish that is made later. Two bows follow as a courteous greeting, as well as two hand claps, to draw the personal attention of the deities. A wish is made in the mind, not spoken out, finished by one bow to thank the deities for accepting the wish.

The three Grand Shrines of the Kumano Kodo (in Hongu Taisha, Hayatama Taisha and Nachi Taisha) play a pre-determined role in the life of the Kumano Kodo pilgrim. At the Kumano Hayatama Taisha Grand Shrine in Shingu, the pilgrim may ask the deities for forgiveness of the sins from his/her past life. At the Kumano Nachi Taisha Grand Shrine, the pilgrim may make wishes for his/her present day life. At the Kumano Hongu Taisha Grand Shrine, the pilgrim may ask for being accepted to heaven in the future.

Grand Shrine of Hong Taisha

Grand Shrine of Hayatama Taisha

Grand Shrine of Nachi Taisha

An **Oji** is a small shrine placed along the Kumano Kodo routes with the purpose of protecting the pilgrim and providing him guidance as to the right path and trail in the direction of one of the three Grand Shrines. These shrines often house small stone statutes, representing princes, or children of the Kumano deities worshipped at the three Grand Shrines. They are the guardians of the pilgrims and provide a place for much needed rest along the hazardous way.

Many Oji are named and marked on the route maps. There are numerous Oji along the Kumano Kodo, but five are considered most prestigious: Fujishiro-oji, Kirime-oji, Inabane-oji, Takijiri-oji and Hosshinmon-oji. These are still important landmarks and in the past were important points of passage to the sacred Grand Shrines. You find the last two named main Oji on the Nakahechi Route.

There are 99 Oji between Kyoto and the Nachi Taisha Grand Shrine, though the number 99 doesn't necessarily mean that there are exactly 99, rather it means that there are many (probably more than 100). The last Oji on this route is in Nachi Taisha.

For today's hiker the Oji rather represent a marker on the stage of the route, though many Japanese pilgrims still see them as a place of worship as well. These pilgrims pay the Oji small coins to thank the guardian for their safety and showing the right path.

Multiple torii in front of an Oji Shrine

A **Kannon** is a Buddhist figure, being represented in many temples as one of the most important deities. A deity is a being that is thought of as holy and sacred. Along the Kumano Kodo trails, most little stone statues represent the Kannon Bodhisattva, the great savior to those suffering and protector of children in the afterlife. In Section 4 of the Kohechi Route, from Totsukawa to Yakio, 33 small stone Kannon statues are placed along the trail. See Chapter 7, Section 4 for more details.

Some of these Kannon statues wear a bib. The bibs are put on the statues by parents who lost children, with the prayer that the Bodhisattva will watch over them. It is a common custom that is often practiced on other Buddhist statues as well.

Kannon Statue   *Wearing a bib*

During your trekking you will pass many sites which used to have **Teahouses** in ancient times. They served as a place for rest, refreshing and information exchange for the pilgrims. Along the Nakahechi Route there is only one building of a former Teahouse still standing, the Kakihara-jaya Teahouse remains at the Akagi-goe section (Section number four of the

Nakahechi Route) At all other sites the constructions have long disappeared and you will be looking at empty plots of land and any remaining stones overgrown by lush green vegetation and moss.

Uenishi Teahouse site   *Kakihara-jaya Teahouse remains*

Friendliness

The Japanese people are extremely friendly and polite to foreigners and to each other. Let me give you some examples from my personal experience.

One late afternoon, after more than 20 kilometers hiking, I was very tired, and did not feel like hiking the last 3 kilometers to my Ryokan. I paused at a gas station, and got in discussion with a young man that spoke reasonably well English. I explained my situation, and immediately he made a phone call to my Ryokan. I heard him speak in Japanese and heard the word 'gajin', which means foreigner, and he looked at my beard as the hotel manager probably asked for a description of my person. Ten minutes later the hotel manager drove up with the hotel shuttle and brought me back to his Ryokan.

At breakfast and dinner, the earlier mentioned short old lady explained all the dishes to me in Japanese, prepared the shabu shabu and cooked the rice for me on my little table. She put the rice in my bowl, and at some point even wanted to show me how to eat the rice with the dry seaweed sheets and put the chopsticks in my mouth.

At the front desk of each accommodation they were extremely helpful in sorting out the bus time tables and connections for my travel for the next day. At one Ryokan, one of the staff even drove me to the bus stop, and later I saw the manager walk more than a kilometer to the same bus stop with several of his Japanese guests.

During my Kumano River Boat Tour, I met an 83-year-old Japanese man, who had a beautifully walking stick, decorated with mantras in Japanese Kanji characters. Despite his age, the man was very fit. He told me that this was his last pilgrimage and that he had completed his tour of the 88 Temples. I had been looking to buy a traditional Kumano Kodo walking stick for several days, and I was so impressed with his walking stick, that I asked him if I could buy it. He refused, but half an hour later told me via the tour guide (who translated in English) that he wanted to give his walking stick to me for free. I was deeply impressed by the generosity of this kind man, and warmly accepted his kind offer.

One day, late afternoon, I arrived at the Tourist Office with a need to recharge my phone battery, which was down to 4%. I did not have my charger with me, so I asked a staff member of the Tourist Office if I could use one of theirs. One staff member had one in his car, and he offered me to take my phone to his car to have it charged there for 30 minutes, which I happily accepted.

Friendly Japanese people

Onsen

Along the Nakahechi and Kohechi Routes there are many locations which have an Onsen, a natural hot spring. Close to Hongu Taisha there are even three locations named Yunomine Onsen, Kawayu Onsen and Wataze Onsen. Each of these locations specialize in the hot spring baths, and most of the Ryokans in these locations have an inside as well as an outside hot bath. These accommodations are very popular with foreign as well as Japanese tourists, so make sure that you book your stay well in advance. In the whole area of the Kii Mountains there are many locations that have hot springs, even when they don't have Onsen in their hotel or location name. The Ryokans with the Onsen are more expensive than those without a hot spring, however, it is worthwhile to book a stay there.

The bathing procedures at an Onsen are rather special. In your room you find two towels, a regular bath towel, though of small size, and a small towel wrapped in a plastic bag. You also find a Yukata (ankle-long cotton bathrobe), quite often in multiple sizes, in a basket in your closet. Before leaving your room, take off all clothing (though you can leave on underwear if you prefer) and put on the Yukata and tie it with the obi band around your waste. In the closet you will probably also find a thick but short (till the waste) wool Yukata, which you can wear over your long cotton Yukata, in case it is cold.

When leaving your room, you slip in the one-size-fits-all house slippers, and with the two towels in your hand, you walk over to the hot spring bath. The bath area is separated for men and women, and the color of the noren (a traditional fabric divider, usually having one or more vertical slits and hanging in front of an entrance), will determine which entrance you have to take. A blue colored noren shows the men's entrance, a red colored noren shows the women's entrance. At most Onsen the noren will be switched at midnight, so that the bathing area is swapped every day.

Behind the sliding entrance door, there is an open shoe cabinet, where you leave your slippers. Barefoot you step on the elevated floor of the changing room, which will have multiple sinks and a rack with open baskets. Sometimes there are no open baskets but instead lockers which can be closed with a key which you take with you in the hot spring bath. You undress and put your Yukata, medium sized towel, and room/safe key in the open basket. The unused baskets are upside-down.

You are naked and take the small towel with you in the bath area. The first thing you will notice, after opening the sliding door to the hot spring, is the smell. There is the distinct smell of rotten eggs, caused by the sulfur odor which comes with the hot spring water from deep in the earth. The hot spring water comes to the surface with a temperature between 60 and 90 degrees Celsius, and is mixed with cold water to achieve a bathwater temperature of around 42 degrees Celsius.

But you can't step in the hot bath yet, first you need a thorough wash. For this purpose, the wall is lined with 'washing stations'. Each small station has a hot/cold water tab, a shower head, liquid body soap, shampoo, a small bucket and a small seat. You can observe that all the Japanese men (and presumable the women as well) sit down on the small seat, and then in a repeating process fill the small bucket with water and empty the bucket over their head and body. Then they soap their hair and body, which they rinse off again by emptying the small bucket. They use the small towel for washing and scrubbing their body. Once all soap is rinsed off, you can enter the hot bath. But where to leave this small towel? The Japanese men resolve this by folding the small towel and putting it on their head while they are in the bath.

The bath itself is shallow, having a depth of maximum 60 centimeters. When you are sitting on your bottom, the water reaches just above your shoulders and your body (till your neck) is submerged, providing super relaxation of your muscles and bones in the 42 degrees' hot water. There is an intermediate step to get into the bath, and when you sit on this step, you can submerge your legs but your upper body stays above the water, which makes it less hot and better to endure.

Some baths are made of wood, some of marble and some of stone, but all show the signs of years of hot spring water and humidity. You won't find the cleanness that you have in your own bath at home, as the many years of humidity and natural minerals contained in the water leave their sediments and traces on the edges of the bath, the overflow areas and the floor and walls.

It is a great way to the end of your day and to relax your muscles strained from the hike in the Kii Mountains. If there is an outside bath, try that one as well, because the Sulfur smell will be a lot less and the area will be a lot less humid, making the hot water temperature more bearable for your bodily circulation.

After the bath, the Japanese men (and presumable the women as well) perform the same washing routine, before getting back to the changing area.

You will see the Japanese, as well as foreign tourists, wear the Yukata at the public areas such as the restaurant and in the hotel as well.

Noren at entrance

Changing room

Inside bath with washing area

Outside bath

Chapter 5

THE HIKING EXPERIENCES

In addition to many of the local traveling and cultural aspects already described in the previous Chapters, there are some further specific topics of interest to the hiker.

On the Hiking Trails

The Nakahechi Route, as elaborately described in Chapter 6, attracts quite a lot of long distance hikers as well as day-tourists. The closer you come to the Hongu Taisha and Nachi Taisha Grand Shrines, the larger the numbers of tourists and pilgrims. Particularly at Nachi Taisha you will encounter bus-loads of tourists. This has four main reasons. Firstly, it is the end of the Kumano Kodo, secondly it contains some beautiful pathways along 800-year-old cedar trees where all the commercial photos for the brochures are taken, thirdly it is easily accessible by road and lastly, this location has Japan's highest waterfall.

In contrast, the Kohechi Route, as extensively described in Chapter 7, attracts hardly any hikers. There are no day-tourists on this 4-day trail, and only the die-hard pilgrims walk this arduous route. During my four days on this trail I only met three elderly Japanese people walking this route. This trail is through isolated mountains and forests with only few access roads;

ideally when you are looking for solitude and tranquility, away from the masses of other people.

In ancient times the male pilgrims used to wear a Yukata in white color. At present, you might come across a few Japanese pilgrims that wear white clothing as well. When you hire a local tour guide, he will most likely wear the typical straw hat, as well as a white outfit. A thousand years ago, the people used to be buried in white clothing, and since the Kumano Kodo was such an extra-ordinary endeavor at that time, the pilgrims used to be dressed in a white colored Yukata in advance, so that they could be buried immediately in case they would perish during their trip.

The panoramic views from the hiking trails of the Nakahechi and Kohechi Routes are beautiful. You see the many green forested mountains with differing shades of green, some covered by clouds, some bright in the sun, some close, some far away. During the months March and April, you will see colorful cherry trees dotted in the green forested mountains, which together with the fresh light-green leaves of the sprouting trees, will be a colorful spectacle on the slopes. From the viewpoints you will see patches of road snaking through the mountains, rivers cutting deep into the mountain valleys, and very small looking houses and cars along the valley roads. Most of the routes are through the dense rain forests, where you are able to admire the forested nature, such as crystal clear little streams coming down the mountain, bamboo forests, moss covered trees and an occasional small pond.

You will hear the chirping of birds, the croaking of frogs, the sounds of silence, the absence of manmade sounds, but you will also hear your heartbeat drumming in your ears as you ascend the steep path.

You will smell the morning dew, the wet leaves after the rain, the pine trees, the timber where trees have been cut, and the humidity of places deep in the forest.

You will feel spider webs that hang between the trees over the path. You get them on your arms and in your face, and you often need to wipe the thin threads away, especially when you are the first one on the trail.

You will come across many different types of under-footing on the Kumano Kodo. The Kumano Kodo guides you on asphalt roads, concrete roads, forest trails with leaves, forest trails with hard dirt, forest trails with bare tree roots, forest trails with steps cut out between rock formations, forest trails with flagstones, or with flagstone steps, forest trails with steps held together by large and small lose rocks, forest trails with steps made out of rounds timber, trails along the beach with small and large rocks, trails over wobbly hanging footbridges, cliff trails that have been washed away by rain or landslide, paths on makeshift wooden footbridges, etc. Kumano Kodo provides a wide variety, and an always changing under-footage, always needing your attention where you place your next step, except for the asphalt and concrete roads of course.

The many flagstones, stones, rocks and timber steps were laid with the intention of preventing the soil to be washed away during the many days of heavy rainfall in the Kii Mountains. At times these stone and wooden steps make the trail easier, but at other times also very difficult because they can be very slippery, uneven or lose, testing your endurance and spirit for completion of your pilgrimage. It is amazing how some parts of these flagstone steps are laid deep in the forests, without any obvious means of getting those large stones there, other than through manual labor or horses a thousand or many hundreds of years ago. It is unclear who laid them or when that was done, but present day, these flagstone steps have become a symbol of the Kumano Kodo trails.

Collecting Stamps

UNESCO links the Kumano Kodo and the Camino de Santiago, as both are listed under the UNESCO World Heritage Pilgrimage Routes. You can read more about their linkage on the website www.spiritual-pilgrimages.com. On each of these pilgrimages you can collect stamps at certain locations, evidencing that you have walked the route leading up to the stamp location. The 'spiritual pilgrimage' organization has developed a booklet in which stamps for both the Kumano Kodo and the Camino de Santiago can be collected, calling it the 'dual pilgrimage'. Pilgrims can send in their stamp book to receive a dual pilgrimage pin badge.

The dual Pilgrimage Stamp book, with two-sided use

The Kumano Kodo side of the booklet has room for 30 stamps, whereas the Camino de Santiago side has room for 40 stamps. There is no requirement to walk the complete routes, it suffices to walk certain parts to collect an adequate number of stamps to qualify for the dual pilgrimage.

On the Nakahechi Route you are able to collect a maximum of 36 stamps, on the Kohechi Route a maximum of 6 stamps. In the following Chapters 6 and 7, you will find details and a photo of the stamps of both routes.

The stamp and red ink cushion can be found in a separate little wooden house on a pole, which looks like a bird house. This is consistent for most part of the routes, but not everywhere. There are some places where they are not in a wooden house or they are in a place which can easily be overlooked.

The Tourist Information Center at the train station of Kii Tanabe can give you a complete list of all stamp locations, which you can use as a checklist on your routes. Searching the stamps and collecting them adds an additional touch to the pilgrimage, one of which feels a bit like a treasure hunt.

Stamplist (with using marks)   *Stamp house*

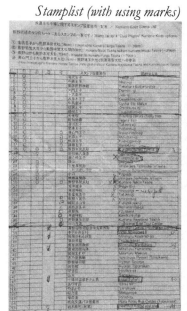 

All stamps from the Nakahechi Route

5 out of 6 stamps from the Kohechi Route

Number of Pilgrims on the Trails

There are no official statistics detailing the number of pilgrims on the Kumano Kodo. The UNESCO World Heritage book states that 15 million people visit the Kii Mountain Range and the sacred Sites and Pilgrimage Routes, each year. However, this number does not represent the number of pilgrims/hikers on the Kumano Kodo routes.

So let me make some estimates myself. The busiest place on the Nakahechi Route is certainly Nachi Taisha, for the four reasons already explained before. Assuming a certain number of tour buses plus other groups and individual travelers, I estimate the number of visitors at around 0.5 to 0.8 million per year. Most people visiting Nachi Taisha, however, arrive by coach, and won't hike the Nakahechi Route, or perhaps just a couple of kilometers 'to get the feeling'.

Based on the number of other hikers that I encountered during my walk on the Nakahechi trails, I estimate the annual number of hikers that do the 2, 3, or 4-day route at around 50'000 to 100'000. This means that the distance between the hiker in front and behind you would be around 250 meters on average. Given the fact that most of the trails are through the forest with winding paths, it means that you won't see the other pilgrim till you get within 50 meters in distance. So you will have the feeling that you are alone on the trail for most of the time, though regularly passing other pilgrims going in the opposite direction. That is consistent with my own experience on most of the Nakahechi Route. As you get closer to one of the three Grand Shrines, the number of hikers will increase, due to the day-tourists trying out a short stretch of the Kumano Kodo as well. The

Nakahechi Route consists of six popular sections and three additional, not so popular, sections. The number of pilgrims walking all sections of this route are probably below 5'000 annually.

Koyasan is a very popular location for tourists as well. Based on the number of Shukubo and the popularity of this destination with tour groups, I estimate the number of annual visitors to Koyasan at around the same level as Nachi Taisha, between 0.5 to 0.8 million. Koyasan provides 52 Shukubo accommodations, whereas Nachi Taisha only has day-trip tourists. It is very likely that many of the tourists visiting Nachi Taisha also visit Koyasan during their travels on the Kii Peninsula.

The number of pilgrims hiking the Kohechi Route is, however, a completely different story. Based on the number of hikers that I encountered during my four days on this route, as well as the other pilgrims I met during my stays in the small villages along the route, I estimate the annual number to be around 10'000, to 20'000. Assumable most hikers on this route will complete the four days. This means that there will be an average distance between you and the hiker in front and behind you of more than 1 kilometer. Given the mountainous and winding trails, it means that you will be alone during the day, perhaps only encountering the occasional hiker going the opposite direction. This matches my personal experience during my four days on this route. As this route is more remote with more difficult access, the likelihood of meeting day-tourists is small.

As already indicated, the above estimates are subjective and need to be taken with caution, but no other accurate and reliable statistics are available. However subjective these estimates are, they are a pretty good indication of what you can expect in terms of 'foot traffic' on these two routes.

According to my observations, the majority of the tourists along the two routes are Japanese, with French and Spanish tourists making up the second largest group, followed by American tourists. There are many French and Spanish tourist groups because of the UNESCO linkage between the Kumano Kodo and the Camino de Santiago, with both listed under the UNESCO World Heritage Pilgrimage Routes.

On a side note, the above estimates make an interesting comparison to the number of pilgrims on the Camino de Santiago. Official statistics put the number of pilgrims that receive the compostelas at the Pilgrims Office in Santiago between 200'000 and 300'000 each year, with the month August spiking at more than 50'000. On average more than 800 pilgrims officially complete their tour each day on the Camino. From a hiker's perspective, that means on average there will be one other pilgrim 25 meters ahead of you, as well as 25 meters behind you. As most of the path is on or along roads, you will have clear visibility on the many people in front and behind you. On top days, such as during summer months, statistically that average distance will decrease to 12 meters. You will be walking in processions with other pilgrims.

If you are looking for the company of other hikers during your pilgrimage, then you will enjoy the Camino de Santiago. If you are looking for solitude during your pilgrimage, you will thoroughly enjoy the Kumano Kodo.

The Weather

Heavy rainfall and strong winds are very common in the Kii Mountains, which have dense temperate rainforests. It is one of the areas in Japan that is most often hit by Typhoons (hurricanes), coming in from the Pacific Ocean, in the period from June to October, but most heavily in August and September. In 2011 a Typhoon caused major damage, flooding and earth slides to many areas in the Kii Peninsula. Look at the following statistics showing the trend line as well as levels of rainfall and temperature. High temperature and high rainfall results in high humidity, which makes hiking more challenging. Whenever you plan your hiking and pilgrimage, you are bound to have one or multiple days of rain. I refer to my experience as described in Chapter 7, Section 4 of the Kohechi route, so come prepared with the appropriate outfit. You may also consider to match your visit to a period where there is less rainfall and lower humidity.

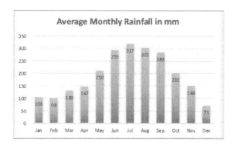

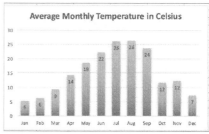

The Cherry trees blossom from beginning of March till mid of April. That is always a special time for admiring these beautiful little, mostly pink colored, flowers on the trees in the forests, along the rivers and the hiking trails.

Tip # 1: *Pilgrim the Kumano Kodo in early Spring time when humidity ana rain fall are at their lowest, ana you can admire the cherry blossoms dotting the landscapes.*

Heavy rainfall

Cherry blossoms

Early morning

Chapter 6

THE NAKAHECHI ROUTE

Summary of the 9 Nakahechi Sections

The Nakahechi Route is the most popular route of the Kumano Kodo, attracting the most tourists and pilgrims. The present day Nakahechi Route usually has its starting point at the Takijiri-oji, which is about 40 minutes by bus from Kii Tanabe (from the West), or about one hour and 25 minutes by bus from Hongu Taisha (from the East). Takijiri-oji is an isolated place in a valley in the mountains, without accommodations, so must be reached by bus or other means of transportation to start your hike.

The Nakahechi Route covers a distance of about 90 kilometers (including ca. 16 kilometers over the Kumano-gawa River) till you arrive at Nachi Taisha.

From Nachi Taisha the pilgrims used a 'shortcut' to get back to Hongu Taisha, and from there on used the same trail back to Tanabe and Kyoto. When you add-in this 'shortcut' to get back to Hongu Taisha, the total length of the Nakahechi trail increases to ca. 118 kilometers (including ca. 16 kilometers over the Kumano-gawa River).

Finally, when you add the additional route from Hongu Taisha to Yunomine Onsen as described in Section 3 and the Section 4 'shortcut' to Yunomine Onsen, you end up with a total trail length of ca. 128 kilometers (including ca. 16 kilometers over the Kumano-gawa River).

The trails take you over several mountain passes, generally ranging between 300 and 600 meters in altitude, with the exception of two passes along the Ogumotori-goe section, which take you to a level of almost 900 meters.

There are good and detailed route maps for all sections, but for Sections 6 and 7 they are only in Japanese. All route maps can be obtained at the Kumano Tourist Offices or online at www.tb-kumano.jp. Accommodations along the route can be easily booked via the Kumano Travel Reservation System (www.kumano-travel.com).

For those pilgrims that want to start their walk in Kii Tanabe, only Japanese language route maps are available (handed out by the Tourist Information Office). The trail from Kii Tanabe station to Takijiri-oji has a length of about 17 kilometers.

The following simplified map links the 9 Sections of the Nakahechi Route in the sequence that the pilgrims would have travelled them a thousand years ago.

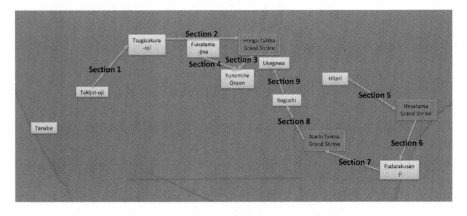

This sequence differs from the modern day promoted routes for foreign tourists in three ways:

1. After having reached Hongu Taisha, many modern day hikers subsequently walk Section 9 followed by Section 8 (opposite direction).

2. Sections 6 and 7 are seldom hiked by foreign pilgrims, as only Japanese language route maps are available. Many foreigners take the bus to reach Fudarakusan-ji and Nachi Taisha.

3. Section 5, the Kumano River Boat Tour, is enjoyed by many tourists as a nice add-on to their stay in the Kumano area, and probably not regard it as an historical part of the Kumano Kodo. In ancient times the route from Hongu Taisha to Hitari would also have been traveled on the Kumano River, but nowadays no such river transport is available, leaving a gap in the ancient Kumano Kodo trail of about 16 kilometers.

Key statistics for the nine Sections of the Nakahechi Route are as follows:

NAKAHECHI ROUTE (all numbers are estimates based on personal experience)	Section 1 Takijiri-oji to Tsugizakur a-oji	Section 2 Tsugizakur a-oji to Kumano Hongu Taisha Grand Shrine	Section 3 Kumano Hongu Taisha Grand Shrine to Yunomine Onsen	Section 4 Funatama-jinja to Yunomine Onsen	Section 5 Kumano River Boat Tour from Hitari to Kumano Hayatama Taisha Grand Shrine	Section 6 Kumano Hayatama Taisha Grand Shrine to Fudarakusa n-ji	Section 7 Fudarakusa n-ji to Kumano Nachi Taisha Grand Shrine	Section 8 Kumano Nachi Taisha Grand Shrine to Koguchi	Section 9 Koguchi to Ukegawa	Total
Walking distance (km)	20.0	24.0	4.2	6.0	1.3	19.0	8.0	15.0	14.5	112.0
Waterway distance (km)					16.0					16.0
Walking time (hrs:min)	5 to 7	6 to 8	1 to 2	1:30 to 2:30	0:30	4 to 6	2:30 to 3:30	5 to 7	4 to 6	29:30 to 42:50
Altitude meters	1700	1700	475	665	150	200	550	1960	1050	8'450
Lowest altitude (meters)	80	90	55	120	0	0	10	60	60	
Highest altitude (meters)	690	670	290	436	125	50	350	883	460	
Stamps	1 to 9	10 to 18	19-20	none	36 to 34	33 to 31	30 to 26	25-24	23 to 21	36
Distance Markers nr. (every 500 meters)	1 to 33	34 to 43 and 50 to 75	1 to 3	1 to 11	none	none	none	1 to 29	29 to 54	
Difficulty (out of 5)	4	5	1	1	0	3	2	5	3	3.6
Percentage of road	30%	30%	25%	0%	80%	90%	70%	8%	9%	36%

When you put the key elements of distance, altitude and altitude meters in a chart, the nine sections can be easily compared to each other, and present a good visualization of the Sections for purpose of your hiking and travel planning.

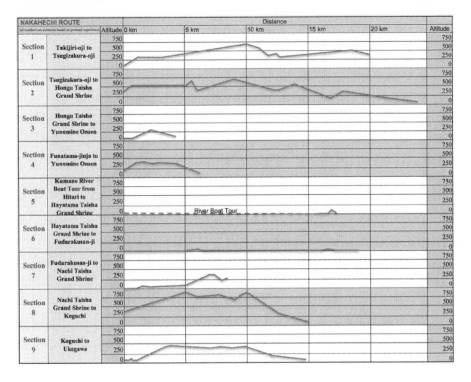

In the subsequent almost 200 pages of this Chapter you will find extensive descriptions of each of the sections supported by over 400 photos.

Section 1: Takijiri-oji to Tsugizakura-oji

Key Data

Walking distance: ca. 20 km
Walking time: ca. 5 to 7 hrs.
Altitude meters: ca. 1'700 meters
Lowest altitude: ca. 80 meters
Highest altitude: ca. 690 meters
Stamps at: Takijiri-oji (1), Nezu-oji (2), Takahara Kumano-jinja (3), Daimon-oji (4), Jujo-oji (5), Osakamoto-oji (6), Gyuba-doji Statue (7), Chikatsuyu-oji (8), Tsugizakura-oji (9).
Markers: 1 to 33
Difficulty: 4 out of 5
Percentage of road: ca. 30%

Kumano Kodo

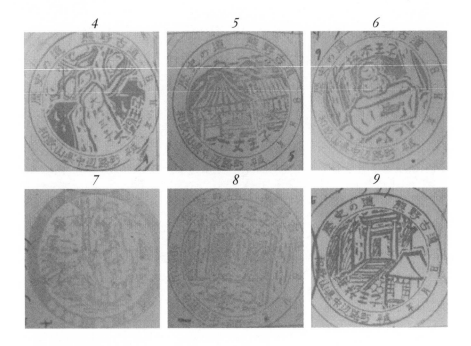

Description of the Section

There are no hotel accommodations at Takijiri-oji, so you need to take the bus to get there, either from Tanabe city or from the area around Hongu Taisha, wherever you have your accommodation.

From the bus stop it is only a few hundred meters, across the bridge, to the Takijiri-oji where a metal plaque, set in a large boulder, commemorates the inclusion of the Kumano Kodo as an UNESCO World Heritage Pilgrimage. Here at this point two rivers converge, the Tonda-gawa main river, and the smaller side river called Ishifune-gawa. Across the street is the Kumano Kodo Pilgrimage and Hiking Center, which provides restrooms, a place to sit, some simple drinks and information about the Kumano Kodo. For most pilgrims the Kumano Kodo starts at this Oji. It is one of the five major Oji shrines and the Pilgrims' access point to the sacred mountains.

The small wooden house on a pole that holds the stamp, is in front of the Oji, on the left side. For most pilgrims this is the first stamp in their stamp booklet, which will bestow both a proud and exciting feeling to have officially kicked-off the pilgrimage. Since ancient times, Takijiri-oji has been considered the entry point to the Kumano Kodo. Takijiri means 'base of the watefall' and is a reference to the converging of the above mentioned two rivers. As indicated in an earlier Chapter, cold water washing rites were practiced to purify the body and spirit during the Kumano Kodo. After the purification, the pilgrims would pray, meditate, and read poetry as part of intense ceremonies for the deities.

The track goes immediately into the forest and up into the mountains. The hike is steep in between trees, sometimes with stone steps, but mostly with natural steps made from rocks and bare tree trunks. Many of the tree trunks show the wear and tear by the many shoes of pilgrims having traversed this route over the years and centuries.

There is one tricky point during the climb, at a junction in the path where the sign post points towards a big rock. On the right side of the rock there is a sign "not Kumano Kodo", and there is no obvious passage. But when you get closer to the large boulder and look towards the left of it, you can see a narrow passage between the Chichi-iwa Rock and another large boulder. Climb through, and you can continue the trail. The large boulder named 'Chichi-iwa Rock has an interesting legend. The story has it that a man named Hidehera Fujiwara was on pilgrimage to Hongu together with his wife, and his wife gave birth to a baby in the small cave on the left side of the giant rock. The baby was left under the cover of the big rock, and survived, because a wolf fed the baby by dripping her milk down the rock. On the return journey, Hidehera and his wife collected the baby and went home. Chichi-iwa literally means 'milk rock'. Passing through the cave on the left side is known as Tainai Kuguri, literally meaning 'passing through the womb'. Superstition has it that women passing through the cave will have an easy birth of their child.

After a short continuation of the climb you arrive at the Nezu-oji, where you can add stamp number 2 in your booklet. The name of this shrine first appeared in a guidebook dating back to the end of the 17th century, so compared to some other shrines is relatively 'young'.

You will still be able to hear the traffic from the main road for a while, till dense forest and hills block out those sounds. The environment becomes very tranquil with only the forest's natural sounds surrounding you. Every 500 meters there are short distance marker-poles along the path. The marker poles display the Nakahechi name of the route, and the marker number, as well as the phone number of the police station and fire station. The marker number starts at 1 at Takijiri-oji and, for the day, finishes at 33 at the Tsugizakura-oji.

After about 45 minutes you reach a lookout point where there is a panoramic view on the Tonda-gawa River valley and the Kii Mountains sloping up on the other side of the river. Here you will have reached your first 'high' altitude at 336 meters, after increasing your elevation by around 250 meters.

For the next two kilometers the terrain becomes flatter and you walk on a forestry ridge, with trees all around. Because of the early time of the year, beginning of April, many of the trees are still without leaves and I can occasionally see the sky and the distant mountains. I can imagine that these forests become even more dense and darker when the trees carry their full leaves.

The trail passes several resting areas, places to sit down and let the legs recover from the climb. As long as the trail is in the forest there are no service points for drinks or food. During this section's hike, you come across three points where the trail crosses a location where service is possible: at Takahara Kumano-jinja, which is 90 minutes after the start, at the Gyuba-doji guchi bus stop 25 minutes before Chikatsuyu-oji and at Chikatsuyu-oji, which is 75 minutes before the end. That means for the longest middle part of the trail, you are in the forest, and you will need a lunch box from the hotel. Drinking water can be obtained from a tap at a number of places along the route, so it is not necessary to carry many liters of water.

Most of the shrines are clearly visible on the path of the Kumano Kodo, however, not all. Before you get to the shrine of Takahara Kumano-jinja, the path follows a normal road with houses alongside. It is easy to walk past this shrine on the right hand side, because it is not near the road and additionally, when I visited, it was partially covered in scaffolding and white plastic for refurbishment. After a 15-minute hike up a steep road past this shrine, I met some people that asked me if I found the previous stamp (number 3). They had walked right past the shrine without noticing it. The little stamp houses at the other locations of the oji shrines are usually easy to find. Of course so long as you know that there is a stamp to be obtained there. So make sure you check the stamp list provided by the Pilgrimage Center or match the stamp requirements to the details in this guide.

Tip # 2: Use the stamp list from the Pilgrimage center as checklist for the locations where you should find stamps.

The Takahara Kumano-jinja, is not one of the 99 Shrines. This shrine was probably constructed in the 15th or 16th century, and contains an image of Buddha fitted on a copper plate. After the Takahara Kumano-jinja, the path goes very steep up the hill via a narrow asphalted footpath. When the path turns into the forest again, it keeps climbing, while you pass a tranquil small pond on your right side. After following the forest trail further up the slope and after a sharp turn to the right, with a steep climb with steps, you arrive at the Daimon-oji for your 4th stamp. The name Daimon means large gate, and in the past a large torii gate of the Kumano Hongu Shrine was located nearby.

About a kilometer and a half further, via a steadily climbing path you come to the Jujo-oji remains, where you put stamp number 5 in your booklet. This shrine is located on an old pass, where, according to documents from the 12th century, there used to be a teahouse and some other stalls.

The trail continues to climb up slowly and more steeply before the highest point of that section, the Uwadawa-jaya Teahouse remains, at ca. 690 meters above sea level. This teahouse was one of many along the pilgrimage route. Teahouses were an important part of the Kumano Kodo infrastructure, offering rest, food and information exchange. This site was used as residence till 1926.

For more than a kilometer the trail subsequently slowly loses altitude, and before reaching the Osakamoto-oji, the trail descents more steeply. At this Oji shrine you obtain your 6th stamp. 12th century legend has it that at the foot of the Osaka pass a pilgrim saw a tall tree with a snake-shaped object. It was said that in the past a woman was transformed into that object.

Stamp number 7 you obtain at the Gyuba-doji statue, which is about a kilometer further downhill, towards the right side of the path, up a small hill. The left statue depicts the Emperor Kazan (968-1008) as a boy riding a horse and cow. The right statue depicts Ennogyoja, the legendary founder of Shugendo, a mixed religion based on mountain ascetic practices. Towards the back there is also a stone stupa monument dating from the 12th century.

After a last steep descent, coming out of the forest, you walk a hundred meters on a road, after which you take a right to continue into the forest on a decline which brings you to the main road in the valley and across the bridge over the river Hiki-gawa, and you've arrived at the Chikatsuyu-oji on your left side. Here you place stamp number 8 in your booklet. The Chikatsuyu-oji is one of the oldest shrines and lies in a valley between mountains, alongside the Hiki-gawa River, where the pilgrims would purify themselves in the cold mountain stream, before worshipping at the shrine. Over 900 years ago, during the peak of the imperial pilgrimages, parties between 200 and 800 people would be accommodated in the area.

The Kumano Kodo path continues on the tarmac road for the next four kilometers, sloping slowly upwards, with a couple of steeper sections, particularly towards the end. But before you get to the end of this section, you pass the Hisohara-oji, where no stamp can be obtained.

At the Tsugizakura-oji you are at the end of Section 1 and you can put the 9th stamp in your booklet. You are now between marker 33 and 34 and this Oji is at an elevation of a little over 500 meters, with nice views over the valley to the right side. In the year 1109, a pilgrim wrote in his dairy that there was a cherry tree grafted on a Japanese cypress at this location, which made the cherry tree famous for hundreds of years. Zakura means cherry tree, so this location is called the cherry tree of Tsugi.

During the day I come across only a few other pilgrims. Most of them are elderly Japanese, single men, couples or small groups of women. There is only an occasional foreign tourist. If you seek some solitude, and don't want to hike in a procession, then this would be ideal for you. Surrounded by the sounds of nature without man-made sounds, the smells of the forest and the flowing of the small streams, are great to stimulate peace of mind. Tranquility is easy to find. Especially beautiful were the blooming blossoms along certain parts of the route, at the edge of the forests, close to or in villages. You will be in awe of the beauty of these soft colored silky small flowers growing in large numbers on the trees.

This section of the trail ends at a location where there are no possibilities for spending the night. Only if you end your hike at Chikatsuyu (four kilometers back), you have a choice of three accommodations, one Ryokan and two Minshuku. So either you end earlier, or walk back, or you take the bus back to your hotel again. I take the bus back to my Ryokan in Kawayu Onsen, and walk an extra 1.2 kilometers down the mountain to get to the bus stop in the valley. The statistic on elevation meters includes my final descent of 132 altitude meters along the road. Bus times are infrequent, so I have a waiting time plus 45 minutes by bus, before I could kick off my hiking shoes.

This route gets a 4 out of 5 in the difficulty rating because of its length and remoteness of the beginning and ending point. The trail itself is not so hard, despite the ca. 1'700 altitude meters, as they are spread out over quite a long distance.

Summary of the day: It takes a long bus ride to get to the starting point of this section, and a long bus ride back from the end, back to my hotel. The route itself is long as well, and has several sections that go up rather steeply, however, not for very long. Approximately 70% of the trail is through the forest with mostly relatively easy sections and it does not go up to a high altitude. There are many interesting oji shrines along the way

Highlight of this part: The excitement of starting your hike through beautiful forests. The panoramic viewpoints along the route. The trees, rocks and path all covered with a layer of moss demonstrating the extremely high humidity at the Osakamoto-oji, where the path follows a small mountain stream.

Low point of this part: The final four kilometers are on the road, and this road climbs up very steeply towards the end, when you are already tired. Because there is no sleeping accommodation in Takijiri or Tsugizakura, you are likely to take a bus to and from these locations. This adds up significantly to the day (two to three hours including waiting time, depending on where you are staying), making it a very long day.

After arriving back at the Ryokan Fujiya in Kawayu Onsen, my body is aching from the strain of this first day hike. Particularly my legs are hurting from the ascents and my knees from the descents. I did cover over 1'700 altitude meters today. Back in my room I quickly change into my Yukata, put on my wooden flip flops and go down to the ground floor to one of the hot springs inside the hotel. The hot natural spring water does wonders for my aching muscles and bones. 20 minutes soaking is sufficient to prevent any muscle ache the next morning. That was quite surprising indeed, as towards the end of my first day hike, I could feel all muscles in my legs ache. The special thing about the location of Kawayu Onsen, is that the cold water of the Oto-gawa River is mixed with the 70 degrees' Celsius water bubbling from deep in the earth through the river bed. There are several small sections in the shallow river that are carved out for bathing.

Tip # 3: Book your stay at one of the hotels with a hot spring, at one of the Onsen (Kawayu Onsen, Yunomine Onsen or Wataze Onsen), and enjoy a muscle relaxant hot spring bath after a strenuous hiking day.

When I finally decided how my next day would look like, in terms of time of my departure, it was already too late for the front desk to make the necessary food arrangements. Not that I was so late with my request, rather the kitchen closes after 7:30 p.m. and only opens again at 6:30 a.m. the next morning. In my case, I went to the front desk at 8 p.m. to ask for a lunch box and breakfast before 6 a.m., so that I would be able to catch the 6 a.m. bus. That would mean that I leave the next day for a full day hike, without any food, and since the trail is through the mountains, probably without possibilities to obtain a meal for breakfast or lunch, that was a 'no go'. So I delay the time of my departure to the 8:30 a.m. bus. At least I have my breakfast at the hotel and the kitchen staff have time to prepare a lunchbox for me.

Tip # 4: Arrange your meal requirements for the next day before 7 p.m.

Photos of the Section

Commemorate stone at the starting point of the Nakahechi Route

Takijiri-oji

Steep up *Tainai Kuguri cave*

Chichi-iwa Rock *Not Kumano Kodo*

Nezu-oji

Bare tree roots

Stone steps

Left to Lookout point

Panoramic view on Tonda-gawa River valley

Straight across the street

Hari Jizo with bib

Steps up   *Jizo*

View before Takahara   *Takahara-jinja easily overseen*

Takahara-jinja under scaffolding

Steep up-hill

View on rice terraces at Takahara

Trail and pond

Steps leading to Daimon-oji

Daimon-oji

Slow incline

Jujo-oji

Koban Jizo

Careful

Pass at ca. 690 meters

Up and down

Keep left

Osakamoto-oji

Descending alongside a small stream

Gyuba-doji Statue

Typical under footing

Relaxed trail path

Through bamboo forest

Blossoming cherry trees

Hiki-gawa River and valley

Chikatsuyu-oji   *Hisohara-oji*

Road between Hisohara-oji and Tsugizakura-oji

Torii to Tsugizakura-oji

Guarding hounds at Tsugizakura-oji

Open bathing place (basin near the screen) in the river in shallow water

Oto-gawa River in Kawayu Onsen, carrying much water after the rain

The outside hot spring bath at Ryokan Fujiya

First course of the pre-set dinner

Section 2: Tsugizakura-oji to Hongu Taisha Grand Shrine

Key Data

Walking distance:	ca. 24 km (incl. official detour)
Walking time:	ca. 6 to 8 hrs
Altitude meters:	ca. 1'700 meters
Lowest altitude:	ca. 90 meters
Highest altitude:	ca. 670 meters
Stamps at:	Hidehira-zakura cherry tree (10), Jagata Jizo (11), Yukawa-oji (12), Inohana-oji (13), Hosshinmon-oji (14), Mizunomi-oji (15), Fushiohami-oji (16), Haraido-oji (17), Kumano Hongu Taisha (18)
Markers:	34 to 43 and 50 to 75 (44 to 49 are skipped because of the detour)
Difficulty:	5 out of 5
Percentage of road:	ca. 30%

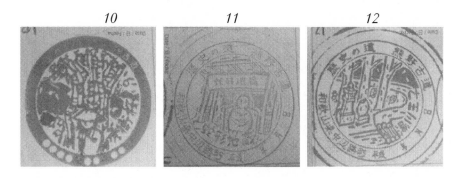

10　　　　　*11*　　　　　*12*

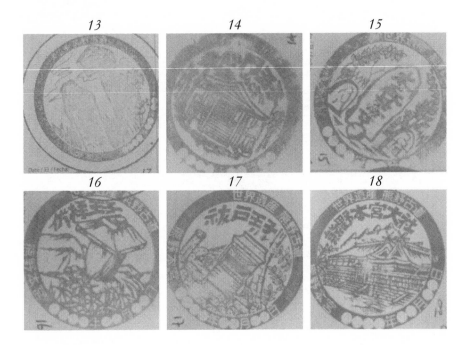

Description of the Section

I need to take the bus again from my Ryokan at Kawayu Onsen to the Nonaka Ipposugi bus stop, taking about 45 minutes to get there. Subsequently it is 1.3 kilometers on an uphill road to get to the altitude of little over 500 meters where the Tsugizakura-oji is situated. Note that the ca. 24 kilometers distance for this section already includes this hike up the hill from the bus stop, as principally no accommodations are available at the location of this starting point, and thus you will have this extra travel time and distance to be added for this route.

From this point, where you left the trail of the previous section, you basically continue on the same asphalt road. After less than one hundred meters you arrive at the Hidehira-zakura cherry tree, where you collect stamp number 10, the first of this section. The little stamp house is on the right side of the road, whereas the cherry tree monument is on the left side. The story of the cherry tree is that Hidehira Fujiwara (the same 12th century pilgrim linked to the chichi-wara rock and cave in the previous section) planted his walking cane in front of the Tsugizakura-oji Shrine in order to pray for the baby's well-being, having left the child behind. The cherry tree grew out of his cane.

The path continues on the road between some houses while gently going up and down, until it changes to the forest trail with steeper sections. You pass the Nakagawa-oji and the Kobiro-oji, before you arrive at the Kumasegawa-oji. According to historical travel dairies, the Nakagawa-oji existed between the 12th and 18th century, but at present there is only a commemorate stone marker left as evidence for its existence. The Kobiro-oji was originally a small Shrine built on the Kobiro pass, which pass disappeared due to modern road construction. The oji was relocated to this spot, but only a part of the stone marker has remained. The Kumasegawa-oji Shrine was first mentioned in a travel dairy in the 13th century. Kumasegawa consists of the words Kumase and gawa. Gawa means river and Kumase is the name of the river which accompanied the ancient pilgrims on their trail to Hongu. Purification would have taken place in this river, before praying at the Shrine. In present day there is no Shrine, only several commemorate stones.

Along the pathways of the Kumano Kodo Routes you come across stone distance markers from the Edo period (1603-1868). The distance between the markers is ca. 3.9 kilometers, and is called one ri. In ancient times, the length of a ri varied, but since the Edo period this has been fixed at 36 cho. One cho is equivalent to ca. 109 meters.

From there the path goes into the forest and becomes a nice trail with easy under footing. The forest trail goes up till you arrive at the Waraji-toge pass at an altitude of around 650 meters. The name Waraji is derived from the traditional woven straw sandals that were used well into the last century and are still worn during traditional ceremonies. The pass carries this name because according to legend, the pilgrims used to change their worn-out straw sandals for new ones at this spot. The straw material wears out quickly, and sometimes does not last longer than a day. Being lightweight and cheap to put together, the ancient pilgrims often carried extra pairs or bought them along their way from locals.

A pretty steep descent on an uneven stone path follows after the pass. About one kilometer later the path is closed and you must follow the detour signs. According to the notice, the old route is blocked because of a major landslide caused by the Typhoon of September 2011. The detour has a length of ca. 4.9 kilometers till you arrive back at the original trail. The extra distance added by the detour is ca. 2.5 kilometers. The detour takes you downhill first, on a forest road following a small river, till you make a sharp left and cross the river to commence a steep climb up. There are many steps and the ascent is without horizontal sections for your legs to recover. There are some nice panoramic views along the climb, but the Iwagami-toge pass is unspectacular, being in the forest without views, at an altitude of ca. 670 meters. The descent is also rather long and steep on forest trails. Before arriving at the Jagata-Jizo, you have a nice trail along a river, after which the path connects with to the original trail again. At this point you also collect your 11th stamp. The Jagata-Jizo is 60 meters to the right of the trail, but the usual Kumano Kodo trail signs point the way. The Jizo is in a small wooden enclosure with a roof and wears a red/white bib. You find the usual offerings in front of the small statue, and the dragon dripping water in the trough on the left side of the Shrine. Clear signs of the high humidity of the region are visible everywhere, as most rocks, tree trunks and even the sign posts are covered with moss.

You continue on the forest trail, partly besides a small stream called Uchiyu River that flows down from the Mikoshi-toge pass, and almost a kilometer later you collect stamp number 12 at the Yukawa-oji. This oji is directly next to the trail, on the left side, and has its typical torii in front of the little wooden structure housing the stone statue. In ancient times this location used to be a resting or overnight place, due to its convenience close to the river, as well as before climbing to the Mikoshi-toge pass.

In the mean time you have climbed again, from the Jagata Jizo at about 400 meters in altitude, you arrive at about 550 meters in altitude at the Mikoshi-toge pass. At the pass level there is an open resting area, along the asphalt road. It is inviting to sit down for a while, use the restroom and enjoy the content of your lunch box.

The following descent is long, at about 3 kilometers, to cover only 300 meters' in altitude difference and basically follows the Otonashi-gawa River. You are walking on a dirt road next to the river on an easy trail, when shortly before the Funatama-jinja, at distance marker 59, you find the sign post for the Akagi-goe section of the Nakahechi Route. Please refer to the description under Section 4 in this Chapter for more details. As the thousand-year-old route did not include the Akagi-goe shortcut to Yunomine Onsen, you should also continue the trail to Hongu Taisha. The Funatama-jinja is on your left side and has three torii under which you access the Shrine. The stone trough on the right side before the torii is overgrown with moss. There is one shed made of corrugated iron walls housing two oji shrines and one wooden house containing a Shinto Shrine.

From the Funatama-jinja it is less than half a kilometer on a nice slowly descending dirt road next to the small mountain stream, to the Inohana-oji. At this oji you put stamp number 13 in your booklet. The oji is only a small stone monument, next to the ri distance marker.

Soon after this oji the trail leaves the dirt road along the Otonashi-gawa River and goes uphill via a steep forest trail for the next kilometer, after which you reach the Hosshinmon-oji. You need to cross a road to get to the oji, and the little stamp house with number 14 is on the right side. The Hosshinmon-oji is one of the most important sites on the Nakahechi Route, marking the most Northern point of the Kumano Kodo trail towards the Grand Shrine in Hongu Taisha. 'Hosshin' means 'spiritual awakening' or 'aspiration to Enlightenment', whereas 'mon' means 'gate', thereby carrying the name of the main gateway towards Hongu for achieving purification and relieve of all sins.

For almost two kilometers you follow the road which goes steadily downhill till you reach the Mizunomi-oji for stamp number 15. This oji is known as a Shrine with a water source, and has a resting place for the modern day pilgrim.

Subsequently the route turns into a forest trail without much ascent or descent for the next kilometer. The trail becomes hard again till you reach the Fushiogami-oji, where you put stamp number 16 in your book. The Fushiogami-oji consists of two stone monuments, and represents the location where in ancient times the pilgrims would get their first glimpse of Kumano Hongu Taisha. 'Fushiogami' means to 'kneel and pray', which is what those pilgrims would do at the sight of their destination. At present the forest obscures the view towards Hongu Taisha, but about two kilometers down the path, there is a viewpoint from where the modern day pilgrim can see the old location of the Grand Shrine.

The path steadily descends till you reach Hongu Taisha, although as usual, there are certain intermediate elevations to be conquered.

When you reach the Sangen-jaya Teahouse remains, you are at the intersection with the Kohechi Route, where the last few kilometers of this route join the Nakahechi Route till you reach Hongu Taisha. I refer to Section 4 in Chapter 7. Approximately a kilometer before Hongu Taisha you come across a sign that suggests a small detour to a view point. It is worthwhile to follow the path of that detour because it is relatively short and the view is magnificent. Sure, a climb and a descent are involved, as is usual along any of the trails, but it is worthwhile to do so. You have a panoramic view on the Kumano-gawa River and the Oyunohara giant torii gateway in the distance. At that location the Kumano Hongu Taisha Grand Shrine was located up to 1889. In those days it was on a sand bank where the Otonashi River and Iwata River converged, whereas nowadays the Grand Shrine is on higher ground. The relocation of the Grand Shrine occurred after a flood destroyed part of the original buildings in the year 1889.

The trail becomes a broad path with many ancient looking stone steps, lined with beautiful tall trees. The last few kilometers are magnificent. On this last stretch of the section, you encounter an increasing number of hikers, the closer you get to Hongu Taisha. Looking at the gear and outfit of some of these people walking the path, it seems that they are just enjoying a walk for an hour or so in order to have "tasted" the path of the Kumano Kodo.

Two hundred meters before the Hongu Taisha Grand Shrine you come across the Haraido-oji, where you get stamp number 17. The Haraido-oji is a small stone statue and represents the last location, before the Grand Shrine, where purification rituals would be held. As already described, a thousand years ago, the pilgrims used to purify their body and spirit by washing themselves in the cold water of the many mountain streams they crossed during their long pilgrimage. As the pilgrim progressed on the trails, and increased the number of times that he washed himself, his level of purification would rise until he was supposed to be completely purified before worshipping at the Hongu Taisha Grand Shrine.

Hence proclaiming it the core of the Kumano Kodo pilgrimage: to undergo the suffering and hardship of the long and dangerous trails, combined with frequent cold water purification of the sins from past and present lives, so that the pilgrim can receive rebirth and rejuvenation from the Kumano deities living in the Kumano Grand Shrines.

You arrive at the Grand Shrine via the back entrance, providing access from the left side to the Grand Shrine. You will find your final stamp for this section, number 18, towards the right side, just at the top of the main stairs. Take your time to look around, after which you can descend the long and steep staircase to the front torii.

On the left side is the Hongu Taisha-mae bus stop, where you can catch the bus to the location of your Ryokan. But before you take the bus back to your hotel, it is worthwhile to visit the Kumano Hongu Heritage and Information Center across the road. They have a lot of information about the trails and the history of the Kumano Kodo in the form of a film, brochures, leaflets, and kind and informative replies to your questions. They can help with booking your next excursion, for example the River Boat Tour as described in Section 5 of this Chapter, or provide help with sorting out bus time tables for your accommodations or any other destinations.

This route gets a 5 out of 5 in the difficulty rating because of the long length of this section, the longest of all the sections of the Nakahechi Route, in combination with the different altitudes of the route. The section has four "peaks" which range between 314 meters and 670 meters in altitude, and the trail goes up and down between these peaks. Unlike at some other sections where there is one longer ascend and one longer descend, the constant going uphill and downhill, make it rather tiring, although the elevations are not that high.

Highlight of this part: The many interesting oji. The trail following a small river and the broad path going down towards Hongu Taisha. The viewpoint on the Kumano-gawa River and the Oyunohara giant gateway about one kilometer before Hongu Taisha.

Low point of this part: The detour adds an extra two and a half kilometers to the already long trek. The steep walk, up the road to get from the bus stop to the starting point at Tsugizakura-oji. Relatively long stretches on the road.

Photos of the Section

Road uphill from the bus stop

Hidehira Zakura cherry tree

Trail on the road

Through the forest to the Nakanogawa-oji

And back on the road

Kobiro-oji remains

Views from the elevated road to the main road nr. 311 in the valley

Steep downhill

Along the Kumase River (note all the moss)

Jizo with bib

Forest trail steep uphill

Kumasegawa-oji remains

Steep uphill

Ri-milestone

Waraji-toge pass

Steep downhill

Detour route

Makeshift detour signs

Steep up and up

And up some more on the detour route

View from the top

The Iwagami-toge pass at ca. 670 meters

Temporary toilets and fresh water towards the end of the detour

Downhill forest trail   *End of detour*

Further down an easy trail

Along the river

Jagata Jizo area

Jagata-Jizo with bib

The dragon dripping water for purification before the prayer

Yukawa-oji with torii and Ri distance marker

The view from the oji towards trail along the small stream

Up and down

At the Mikoshi-toge pass ca. 550 meters

Typical Nakahechi Route 500-meter distance marker

Downhill along the little stream

Good trails

Cleaned up after landslides

Typical signpost

Stone steps down

Hard road along the Otonashi-gawa River

Funatami-jinja

The small Shrine with bell

Inohana-oji remains with stamp house

Trailing down

Hosshinmon-oji

Fushiogami-oji remains

Trailing up again on steps and roots

Distant view on Oyunohara, where the Grand Shrine used to be

Haraido-oji

Path trailing down to the final road

Back-entrance to the Grand Shrine

Steep stairs of the front entrance

Gate to the Grand Shrine

Kumano Hongu Taisha Grand Shrine

Temple

Purification

Lights at front entrance

131

Entrance square along main road nr. 168

Section 3: Hongu Taisha Grand Shrine to Yunomine Onsen

Key Data

Walking distance: ca. 4.2 km
Walking time: ca. 1 to 2 hrs
Altitude meters: ca. 475 meters
Lowest altitude: ca. 55 meters
Highest altitude: ca. 290 meters
Stamps at: Oyunohara (19), Yunomine-oji (20)
Markers: 1 to 3
Difficulty: 1 out of 5
Percentage of road: ca. 25%

NAKAHECHI ROUTE				Distance					
all distances are estimates based on personal experience	Altitude	0 km	5 km	10 km	15 km	20 km		Altitude
Section 3	Hongu Taisha Grand Shrine to Yunomine Onsen	750 500 250 0						750 500 250 0

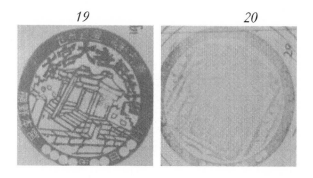

19   *20*

Description of the Section

Thousand years ago, the pilgrims would often pass the Grand Shrine in Hongu Taisha and head straight for Yunomine Onsen, over a section of the Kumano Kodo called Dainichi-goe. Yunomine Onsen has natural hot springs where the pilgrims used to clean up and recover after a long, difficult and dangerous trekking through the Kii Mountains. They would head back on the Dainichi goe section the next day to visit the Grand Shrine in Hongu Taishi.

Up to 1889, the Grand Shrine was on an island in the Kumano River, at the present location of the Oyunohara. As present day pilgrim, you cross the street at the lower entrance of the Grand Shrine complex, towards the Kumano Kodo Tourist Information and Heritage Center, and walk past it towards the huge concrete torii at the end of a straight road. You have seen this torii before, at the end of Section 2, when you took the short detour to the viewpoint close to the end of the trail. You pass through the gate and continue between the large trees on a park lane towards the Oyunohara. There you can collect your first stamp (nr. 19) for this route. Walk up the few steps and cross the grass field with monuments on both sides in a park-like area. At the end turn right on the gravel path, and over the bridge over a small stream till you arrive at the main road nr. 168. There you turn left for a few hundred meters till you see signs to go to the right for the head of the Dainichi-goe trail.

The trail head is on your left hand side, and immediately goes up pretty steep via steps and stones. Note the warning sign for poisonous viper snakes at the start of the trail. Indeed, a snake crossed my path a few hundred meters later. You only have one hill of almost 300 meters to conquer, while the trail passes some huge cedar trees. On the climb up you pass a shrine named Tsukimigaoka-jinja, offering two closed wooden structures and a stone monument. Right after the top you see the Hanakake Jizo on your right side. There are two stone monuments: one rectangular flat stone with inscriptions covered with dirt and moss, and one large, moss covered boulder with two jizo figures carved into the surface of the rock. The carved rock has a large cedar tree growing on top of it. The descent is about as steep as the climb, but you arrive at Yunomine Onsen relatively quickly. Very shortly before getting to the road number 311 in the village, you pass the Yunomine-oji. There you collect your second stamp (nr 20) for this route.

Do as the pilgrims did, a thousand years ago, and spend the night in Yunomine Onsen (founded 1'800 years ago, one of Japan's oldest hot spring resorts). There are only 14 accommodations in the small village, of which two are Ryokans, and the remainder are Minshuku. I stayed at Ryokan Adumaya and enjoyed the hot spring bath (inside as well as outside) of the hotel to relax and recover. Yunomine Onsen is famous for its healing hot springs carrying natural minerals from deep in the earth to the surface at a temperature of around 60 to 90 degrees Celsius. Apart from the 14 accommodations on both sides of the small stream, the little village has a Temple (the Yunomine-chaya Toko-ji Temple), three small public baths and one small tourist/convenience store and one small bar/restaurant. The small stream runs through the middle of the village, next to the only small road, from North to South.

There is a tiny hot spring bath, which is the only hot spring bath registered as a UNESCO World Heritage, under the name Tsuboyu Bath, originating in the beginning of the 12th century. This hot spring is centered around the ancient faith that all diseases can be cured by the deities of Kumano. It is a public bath, and so tiny that only one or two people can use it at a price of 770 Yen ($7.25) for private use for 30 minutes. The use of soap and shampoo is not allowed. The small cabin of the Tsuboyu Bath is made from worn wood and is in the middle of the small stream. There is a second area down at the level of the stream, where locals created a cooking basin (called the Yuzutsu Public Onsen Cooking Basin) in the hot water next to the river. The local people put eggs, vegetables and other food in the basin where the food is heated by the 90 degrees Celsius hot spring water. All along the stone and concrete river bench you see hot pipes transporting the hot spring water to other locations. The many minerals contained in the hot spring water leave their sediment on many places around the hot pipes. The Sulfur smell coming up with the hot water from deep in the earth can't be missed by your nose.

Since this route is rather short, you can consider to attach this to the Tsugizakura-oji to Kumano Hongu Taisha Grand Shrine Section 2, as described above. Alternatively, if you want to have a relaxing day and do some local sightseeing, you can also consider to take the bus to Hongu Taisha and walk back via this route. Or since this route is so short, you could also walk from Yunomine Onsen to Hongu and back again on this same trail.

This route gets a 1 out of 5 in the difficulty rating because it is short with a limited number of altitude meters. It is nice as an add-on to another route, or simply as part of a relaxing and easy day.

Highlight of this part: The beautiful trees in the park lane of Oyunohara. The huge cedar trees at the beginning of the trail. The hot springs of Yunomine Onsen.

Low point of this part: none.

Photos of the Section

World's largest torii at Oyunohara

Park Lane to Shrine

Oyunohara Shrine

Park with several monuments on the sides

Exit of the park to road nr. 168

Follow the sign to the trail head

Snake warning   *Steep steps*

Steady incline of the trail

Tsukimigaoka-jinja

Further up   *Inscribed stone*

Hanakake Jizo   *Descent through carved rocks*

Easy trail   *End in sight*

Yunomine-oji   *Outdoor bath at Ryokan*

Indoor bath at Ryokan

Washing area in indoor bath

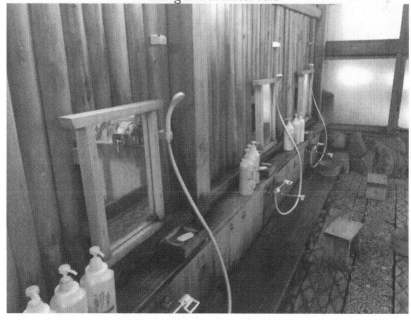

Second course of dinner served in the room

The center of Yunomine Onsen

Tsuboyu Bath

Temple

Temple

Public cooking basin in hot spring water

A Jizo with bib on the river bench

Section 4: Funatama-jinja to Yunomine Onsen

Key Data

Walking distance:	ca. 6 km
Walking time:	ca. 1:30 to 2:30 hrs
Altitude meters:	ca. 665 meters
Lowest altitude:	ca. 120 meters
Highest altitude:	ca. 436 meters
Stamps at:	none
Markers:	1 to 11
Difficulty:	1 out of 5
Percentage of road:	ca. 0%

NAKAHECHI ROUTE			Distance					
		Altitude	0 km	5 km	10 km	15 km	20 km	Altitude
		750						750
Section	Funatama-jinja to	500						500
4	Yunomine Onsen	250						250
		0						0

Description of the Section

Since many hundreds of years, this section called Akagi-goe, was used as a shortcut to Yunomine Onsen. Pilgrims on the Nakahechi Route wanted to go to the hot springs of Yunomine Onsen before visiting the Grand Shrine in Hongu Taisha, as already explained in Section 3. Instead of completing the route to Hongu Taisha and then continuing to Yunomine Onsen, a short cut was created. According to history, this Akagi-goe route was first mentioned in the 16th century. That probably means that this short cut route was created some 500 years after the start of the Kumano Kodo.

This shortcut leaves the trail of Tsugizakura-oji to Kumano Hongu Taisha Grand Shrine as described in Section 2, after the descent from the Mikoshi-toge pass, and shortly before the Funatama-jinja Shrine. To continue to Hongu Taisha and then to Yunomine Onsen via the Dainichi-goe section involves a path with a length of around 12.3 kilometers. The Akagi-goe section brings the pilgrim to Yunomine Onsen in about 6 kilometers, resulting in a shortcut of around 6.3 kilometers, or 51%. In our present day of good roads and trails, good equipment and safety, this may not seem as much, but I can imagine that in the environment of 500 hundred years ago, such a reduction in travel distance and time would have been substantial.

If you have your accommodation in Yunomine Onsen, it is easy to take the Ryujin bus, without transfer, to the Hosshinmon-oji bus stop (520 Yen, $4.90). The bus makes this direct route several times each day, so ask the front desk of your hotel for the times. From the Hosshinmon-oji it is ca. 1.5 kilometers (all downhill) to the junction of the trail, leading to the trail head of the Akagi-goe section. If you stay at another location, just coordinate with the front desk of your hotel for the connections and times of the buses to the Hosshinmon-oji bus stop, as well as the bus times from Yunomine Onsen back to the place where you are staying.

You can of course also hike this section in opposite direction, starting at Yunomine Onsen. You can also combine this section of ca. 6 kilometers with other sections. A nice day trip could for example be to start in Yunomine Onsen (in case you have your hotel there), walk the Akagi-goe section, then at the end of this trail continue to Hongu Taisha, and from Hongu Taisha walk back via Section 3, the Dainichi-goe route. This would make a day trip of around 18.3 kilometers in relatively easy terrain through beautiful forests along ancient trails. You can of course also hike this circle in the other direction, starting first with the Dainichi-goe section and finishing with the Akagi-goe section.

The route described below starts at the junction close to the Funatama-jinja Shrine and finishes at Yunomine Onsen, in the direction that the pilgrims would have walked it 500 year ago.

At the junction in the forest (distance marker 59), follow the signpost and cross the small bridge over the Otonashi-gawa River. The trail starts with a very steep ascent followed by a slow uphill slope till the highest point at ca. 436 meters is reached. This point is already reached after ca. 2.2 kilometers out of the ca. 6 kilometers of the route. There are some good viewpoints to your left side at the higher levels of the trail.

At the highest point you find the Nabeware Jizo, which statue was erected in 1803. 'Nabeware' means 'cracked pot' and the Jizo derived its name from the story that, on this location, in the 13th century a servant made a clay pot crack on the fire while cooking rice, after all the water had evaporated.

Immediately after the highest point there is a rather steep but short descent. The path then trails rather evenly till you see a small shrine containing a statue of Kobo Daishi, the founder of Shingon Buddhism in Koyasan, early 9th century. Please refer to Chapter 7, where Koyasan, as starting point of the Kohechi Route, is described in more detail. About 50 meters after the statue you get to the Kakihara-jaya Teahouse remains. As an exception to the many other Teahouse remains along the Kumano Kodo trails, there is actually still an abandoned building standing at this location. This Teahouse was first mentioned in historical documents during the Edo Period (1603 – 1868) and was still in use till the mid 1970s.

The trail continues on the right side of the remains, but it increases in altitude again to ca. 363 meters. Subsequently the trail slowly descends till you get to a stone signpost. This signpost is a 57-centimeter high rock pillar which has a hand carved into its surface, with a finger pointing the way the Yunomine Onsen. According to an inscription, the stone signpost is from the year 1855.

From there is goes down relatively steep till you reach Yunomine Onsen. The most part of this descent is on stones, which are chaotically placed on the path, making it quite difficult to step from rock to rock. Before you reach the street, the smell of sulfur is already coming your way.

At the end of the trail in Yunomine Onsen (immediately to your left), there is a large boulder sized ca. 2.8 to 2.4 meters, about 3 meters higher than the street level, where according to the belief Ippen Shonin made an inscription in the rock with his finger nails. Ippen Shonin is one of Japan's famous holy figures who reached enlightenment in the 13th century Hongu Taisha. The inscription in the rock is in Bonji characters. These are ancient characters once used to write Sanskrit and here represent the names of Buddhas and Bodhisattvas.

During this short trek I did meet several other hikers. Most were young people, who apparently wanted to try out a short trek, because they were not dressed for long distance hiking.

This route gets a 1 out of 5 in the difficulty rating because it is short with a limited number of altitude meters. Only the beginning and end sections are steep, but the large stretch in the middle is gently sloping up and down.

When this route is combined with another route as suggested above, the difficulty rating of the complete combined route of course changes. That rating will increase because of its length, not because of the steepness, difficulty of the path or high number of altitude meters.

Highlight of this part: beautiful view from the higher parts of the route.
Low point of this part: none

As described at the end of the previous section, it is worthwhile to stay at an accommodation in Yunomine Onsen. I also stayed at Ryokan Yunominesou, which is a bit outside the village towards the South. It is a relatively large accommodation and has a wonderful hot spring bath, indoor as well as outdoor (the largest in the area). As an exception to most other local accommodations, the owner and his staff speak English very well, making communication easy. The pre-set meals for dinner and breakfast are consumed in their central restaurant, where a table is reserved and the food pre-set.

Photos of the Section

Follow the signpost

Take trail to the left

Steep up

Even continuation

Easy trail

Clear panoramic views

Nabeware Jizo   *Trail going down*

Descending to Kobo Daishi Statue

Kakihara-jaya Teahouse remains

Wonderful view

Trailing down with a view

Hand sign

Steep down through rock formations

Left the end of the trail, right the Ippen Shonin rock and monuments

Table reservation by room nr *Outdoor hot spring bath*

Section 5: Boat Tour from Hitari to Hayatama Grand Shrine

Key Data

Walking distance:	ca. 1.3 km, plus distance by boat ca. 16 km
Walking time:	ca. 30 minutes
Altitude meters:	ca. 150 meters
Lowest altitude:	ca. 0 meters
Highest altitude:	ca. 125 meters
Stamps at:	River Boat Tour Operator (36), Kumano Hayatama Taisha Grand Shrine (35), Kamikura jinja Shrine (34).
Markers:	none
Difficulty:	0 out of 5
Percentage of road:	ca. 80%

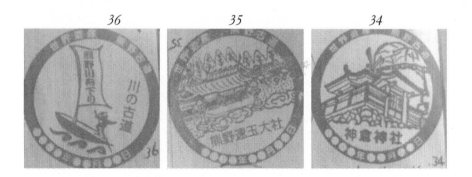

Description of the Section

Thousand years ago the pilgrims took the boat on the Kumano-gawa River (gawa means river in Japanese) from the Kumano Hongu Taisha Grand Shrine to the Kumano Hayatama Taisha Grand Shrine (in Shingu city). Both Grand Shrines are situated next to the river, providing the pilgrims a seamless and effortless connection between the two Grand Shrines. Compared to the walking routes through the mountains, this river descent by boat must have been a great relieve of hardship, however, not for all pilgrims. Thousand years ago, the Emperor, royalties and rich people took the boat. Their servants and the normal pilgrims walked along the riverbank to the Pacific Ocean. It is only during the Edo period (after 1600) that common people were able to take a boat as well. After disembarking, before the river reaches the Pacific Ocean, they walked the last 200 meters to the Grand Shrine. This waterway pilgrimage was mostly in use from the 10th till the 17th century.

Nowadays, the river between Hongu Taisha and Hitari can't really be traveled by boat because of too low water levels. The low water levels are caused by the 11 dams, being used for power generation, that are upstream from Hongu Taisha. The three large dams and eight small dams control the water flow, causing the low levels of the river. In order to provide present day pilgrims and tourists the experience of this ancient part of the Kumano Kodo, a River Boat Tour was put in place in September 2005, one year after the listing of the Kumano Kodo as the UNESCO World Heritage Route. This boat tour starts in Hitari and ends close to the Kumano Hayatama Taisha Grand Shrine, covering a distance of ca. 16 kilometers. Hitari is about halfway down the river from Hongu Taisha, from where the boats descend from a level of ca. 34 meters to sea level. This part of the Kumano-gawa river is registered under the UNESCO World Heritage as a waterway pilgrimage route.

The current boats are similar to those used by the pilgrims a thousand years ago. They are the traditional wooden flat-bottom boats, occupied with one captain, a tour guide and up to eight passengers. Thousand years ago it would take the royalty about four hours to get from the Hongu Taisha Grand Shrine to the Hayatama Taisha Grand Shrine, and about eight hours back upstream. For going downstream, they used the currents and rowers, for going upstream they used special sails for when the wind from the Ocean would blow inland as well as rowers and ropes which were pulled from the shore. Nowadays the flat-bottom boats are moved by a small engine.

The river tour costs 3'900 Yen ($36) for an adult and needs to be booked one day in advance, which can be done at any tourist information center, for example at the train station of Shingu, or at the Kumano Tourist Office in Tanabe or Hongu Taisha, or even at the front desk of your accommodation or online at www.kumano-travel.com. There are two daily times for the regular service departing at either 10 a.m. or 2:30 p.m. The tour takes an hour and a half to get from Hitari to Shingu City. It is easiest to get to the starting point of the River Tour by public bus. Bus number 4 takes 50 minutes from the bus stop of Hongu Taisha-mae to the bus stop Hitari. In case you have your hotel in Shingu, bus number 3 arrives at the Hitari bus stop 30 minutes after leaving Shingu Station. Details of the bus schedules can be found online at www.tb-kumano.jp or at the before mentioned locations where you also book your tour. The bus schedules do not provide a seamless connection with the tour schedule of the river boats, resulting in a waiting time between 30 and 90 minutes, depending on where you come from and whether you have the morning or afternoon tour. The waiting time in the afternoon can, however, easily be used to talk to the friendly tour guides, and relax at the information and seating area in the office of the tour operator. There is also a small supermarket next door to their office, which makes it easy to buy some drinks or snacks to bridge the waiting period.

Be aware that this office also has a stamp for your pilgrim booklet. It is stamp nr. 36, called Traditional Boat Tour Center. When you ask the tour guides, they will show you. But make sure you ask about the stamp while you are still in the waiting area in their office.

The people from the River Boat Tour Office are super friendly. The tourist guide came to pick me up at the bus stop; when I got off the bus, she was already waiting for me. From the bus stop it is a 2-minute walk to their offices, and for the trip to the boat, the tourists are transported by minivan. It takes less than 10 minutes to drive to the place at the Kumano-gawa River where the boats are moored, their bough partly on the stony shore. Before embarking the small flat-bottom wooden boat, you put on a life-jacket and a straw Japanese hat. The boat has four rows of planks with two cushions each, catering for eight guests, plus the captain at the engine at the back and the tour guide with a loudspeaker in the front. The tour guide asks each of the tourists to take a large plastic foil and cover the legs, ensuring that clothing stays dry in case of water spraying from the currents. On the water it can be chilly, and you will need a sweater or jacket, depending on the time of year.

Tip # 5: The wind on the river can be cold, so depending on the time of year, bring a jacket or sweater.

Along the 90-minute tour, the guide explains many points of interest:
The Nunobiki Waterfall is the highest waterfall along the tour. The name means 'cloth stretched out for drying' which is resembled when the waterfall appears white when it carries a lot of water after heavy rain. Because the waterfall carries little water, it is not that spectacular.

The New Waterfall, which emerged after a Typhoon in 2010, is also relatively small, certainly when compared to the high waterfall of Nachi Taisha (I refer to section 7 of this Chapter).

The Aoi Waterfall is named after the emblem of the Tokugawa family, but it is difficult to make out its shape.

The Senjigaeri point is an area along the river embankment which is blocked by rocks and steep passages and in the old days was very difficult to cross for the people accompanying the river barges on foot.

The Nabiki Rock shows how the former Ocean floor has risen diagonally through the movements of the tectonic plates.

Hone Island has a large and long white rock formation, of which a tale says that it represents the severed spine of a demon that was struck down by local gods. At this location, about one third into the tour, the tour guide lets the tourist disembark for taking some photos with the white rocks.

The Tsurigane Rock is overhanging and according to the tour guide resembles a bell. Story has it that if this rock falls, the world would end.

The Hisetsu Waterfall is considered the highlight of views along the tour, however, because of the far away distance and the low level of water coming down the mountain, it is not an obvious a highlight.

Hiru Island is a rock island in the middle of the river, of which it is said that the local gods had their lunch there and played board games.

The underside of a bridge on a side-river, about 40 meters above the current river level, is full with drift wood that is stuck in between its iron beams. During the Typhoon in 2011, the water level rose so high, that drift wood floating on the river surface got stuck underneath this bridge. This is a clear sign of how disastrous this Typhoon must have been and the enormous amounts of water caused by the rain and storm.

The Chihoga-Mine Peak is a ca. 250 meters high forested mountain. The Hayatama Grand Shrine is at the foot on the other side, and the Kamikura-jinja Shrine is halfway up at other side.

The Tatami Rock shows the same geological formation as the Nabiki Rock, and got its name because it looks like tatami mats piled on top of each other, while leaning to the right side. At this point the boat slows down and stays stationary, while the tour guide plays a soft tune on her bamboo flute.

The tree-covered Mifune Island is where according to local legends the deities first appeared, and the boat circles this island.

Along the way of the tour the water is extremely murky and you cannot see five centimeters into the water. This is caused by the sediment being transported from the dams. When the captain guides the boat into a side river, without dams, the water is suddenly crystal clear and you can see the bottom, like through a glass floor.

There are no bridges over the Kumano-gawa River between Hitari and the stop at the Hayatama Grand Shrine. Since this part of the river is considered a cultural heritage route, no construction is allowed. There are however bridges between Hongu Taisha and Hitari, and also immediately after the arrival point at the Hayatama Grand Shrine, a broad traffic bridge can be seen.

After disembarking on the rocky shore of the Kumano-gawa River, it takes only 200 meters to reach the Kumano Hayatama Taisha Grand Shrine. This Shrine is said to have been built in the 9th century. Shingu derives its name from this Shrine. 'Shin' stands for new and 'gu' stands for Shrine in old Chinese. The stamp nr. 35 for your booklet can be obtained at the right end of the building selling the religious and tourist products. This building is directly on the left side, opposite of the Grand Shrine.

The Grand Shrine is a long building set in bright orange, white and green colors, very different from the dark brown wood of the Grand Shrine at Hongu Taisha. Not only the Grand Shrine, but also all other buildings and gates and torii are painted in the same colors, making it look like one integrated complex of buildings. The belief is that a matchmaking deity is housed in this Grand Shrine, attracting many present day people to pray for finding a good match for their life's partner.

The area has a Podocarpus Nagi tree, estimated to be more than a 1'000 years old, which is considered a natural monument in itself. The information tables around this tree are only in the Japanese language, so look out for a tree with a wide trunk, surrounded by a square fence of concrete poles. You find the tree opposite of the small museum, on your left hand side when coming from the main entrance.

According to old traditions, the pilgrims used to visit an even older second shrine close to the Grand Shrine. It is called the Kamikura-jinja Shrine and can be reached by walking about 20 minutes on several small roads passing through residential areas. From the torii at the entrance at the level of the road, there is an extremely steep climb on large steps made of uneven rocks. According to locals, there are 538 steps, but because of the unevenness, it would be very difficult to determine the exact number of steps. Be careful on these steps, they are extremely steep, particularly when descending they can be dangerous. From the Kamikura-jinja Shrine you have a nice panoramic view over Shingu City and the Pacific Ocean in the distance. According to legends, three deities of the Kumano Grand Shrines first descended from the heavens on the great sacred rock called 'Gotobiki-iwa', next to which this shrine is built. This location is one of the most holy places in the Kumano region, being the original Hayatama Shrine. The giant rock has been worshipped for many centuries and excavations found bronze bells from the 3rd century as well as Buddhist Sutras (texts) from the 12th century.

According to the list of stamps and the Japanese language trail guide, stamp number 34 should be available at this location. However, I can neither find a stamp house nor a stamp, not at the torii entrance at street level, not at the level of the Shrine. When I am at the Hongu Taisha Tourist Information Center several days later, they acknowledge that this stamp might not be there. However, they have the same stamp in their Tourist Center and put this stamp in my booklet.

Tip # 6: When at the Tourist Information Center in Hongu Taisha, and you have already visited the Kamikura-jinja Shrine, or you intend to visit this Shrine, have them put stamp number 34 in your booklet.

Call # 2: The Tourist Information Center in Hongu Taisha should make sure that stamp nr. 34 is well visible and permanently obtainable at the Kamikura-jinja Shrine.

You will have noticed that the numbering of the stamps jumps from 20 (at Yunomine-oji) to 36 (at River Boat Tour operator). That is because the official Tourist Office stamp list (I refer to Chapter 5) does not follow the historically correct direction and section sequence of the Nakahechi Route. For Sections 5 to 9, the stamp list follows the opposite direction of the route, tracing the stamps from Ukegawa to Koguchi to Nachi Taisha to Fudarakusan-ji to Hayatama Grand Shrine to the River Boat Tour operator. A thousand years ago, pilgrims traversed this route in the direction from the Kumano River to the Hayatama Grand Shrine, then onwards along the coast to Fudarakusan-ji, then inlands to Nachi Taisha. Originally the pilgrims took this same route back, some 800 years ago though, a 'short cut' route from Nachi Taisha to Hongu Taisha developed, and the pilgrim walked the route via Koguchi to Ukegawa to Hongu Taisha. The stamp list should follow the historically correct direction of Sections 5 to 9, in which sequence these are also described in this travel guide.

Call # 3: The sequence of the stamps between the River Boat Tour center (nr. 36) and Ukegawa (nr. 21) should be reversed in the Kumano Kodo Stamp list to adjust to the historically correct sequence of the pilgrimage route.

This route gets a 0 out of 5 in the difficulty rating because it is mostly relaxing and enjoying the river boat tour. When arriving at the Hayatama Grand Shrine it is easy to continue to the Kamikura-jinja Shrine. The climb from the entrance is via 538 very steep steps, but those are the only sweat-breaking activities in this section of the Nakahechi Route.

Highlight of this part: extremely friendly tour staff and the tour down the Kumano-gawa River and a relaxing day without intensive hiking.

Low point of this part: chilly wind on the river (it was the beginning of April; in the heat of summer the wind might be a nice refreshment).

Photos of the Section

Waiting area at the Tour Operator Office

By minivan to the rocky shore of the Kumano-gawa River

Nunobiki Waterfall   *Nabiki Rock*

The flat-bottom tour boat

Senjigaeri point

Tour guide telling exciting stories

Hone Island

Captain waiting while the tourists look at Hone Island

Kumano-gawa River

Tsurigane Rock

Driftwood stuck under the bridge

Hiru Island

Kumano-gawa River

Tatami Rock

Disembarkation

Front entrance to the Hayatama Grand Shrine Complex

Torii *Purification basin*

Access gate to Grand Shrine

The Grand Shrine

The Grand Shrine

Stamp nr. 35 on the right side counter

The Grand Shrine

1'000-year-old Nagi tree on the left

Torii at the entrance of 538 steps to Kamikura-jinja

The Kamikura-jinja with the Gotobiki-iwa Rock

View over Shingu and the Pacific Ocean

Section 6: Hayatama Taisha Grand Shrine to Fudarakusan-ji

Key Data

Walking distance:	ca. 19 km
Walking time:	ca. 4 to 6 hrs
Altitude meters:	ca. 200 meters
Lowest altitude:	ca. 0 meters
Highest altitude:	ca. 50 meters
Stamps at:	Koyazaka (33), Hamanomiya-oji (32), Fudarakusan-ji (31)
Markers:	a few in Shingu, but none numbered
Difficulty:	3 out of 5
Percentage of road:	ca. 90%

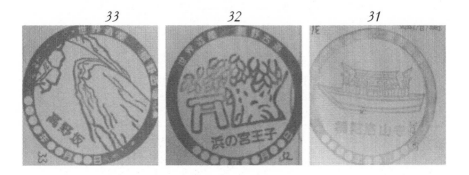

Description of the Section

The route starts at the Hayatama Taisha Grand Shrine from where markers in the pavement guide you through Shingu City. The route guides you first parallel to the Kumano-gawa river, which however can't be seen from where you walk, as buildings block the view. After 10 minutes you come to a first Shrine, which looks like a small edition of the Grand Shrine. It has the same building style and uses the same colors.

Continuing another 30 minutes through the city, you arrive at the Hama-oji Shrine, which is dedicated to the god of the Ocean, Suijin. Its housing is of a simple wooden structure, in wood colors, not as colorful and flashy as the previous Shrine.

From there the pavement markers end. Apart from an occasional signpost along the route, there are no other markers which tell you that you are on the right path.

You cut through a small park, and subsequently you walk for about 2 kilometers along the beach. The Japanese map actually shows this as a paved road or path, which is correct for the first half, but not for the second half. The first half of the path along the Pacific Ocean is an elevated concrete path, behind a meter-high Tsunami protection wall. There are Tsunami warning shields every 500 meters, but no Kumano Kodo markers. Halfway this stretch, the elevated concrete path ends, and the trail continues on the beach. The beach is about 100 meters broad and covered with small and big pebbles. Walking there is rather difficult, and you have to be careful not to twist your ankle on this uneven path. Walking along the wave line is not convenient either, as it is slanted. The best path is midway the beach where the rocks are smallest. There the rocks are mixed with sand, so it is unavoidable to get sand and small pebbles in your shoes. When you look ahead you can see that the beach ends at rock formations protruding into the Ocean. According to the Japanese route map, there is an exit to the right just before these rock formations. The path along the beach has the railway tracks on the right side, so you are boxed in by the Ocean and the Railway tracks. Arriving at the end of the beach, there is indeed a tunnel under the railway tracks where a narrow path along a stream guides you away from the beach to the other side of the railway tracks. At the other side of the tracks there is a memorial poster with a description of the significance of this location in Japanese. The location is called Koyazaka, and its significance lies in the sloping up the hill of this coastal path which the pilgrims had to traverse thousand years ago. Three small stone statues mark this location. The little house with the stamp is there as well, and you can place stamp nr. 33 in your booklet.

The Japanese route map does not make a distinction between paved and unpaved road; according to the map all the 19 kilometers of route are paved. This makes reading the map a bit difficult, because from the Koyazaka location, the trail continues through a forest and up a hill, basically parallel to the railway tracks. After little over a kilometer you get to a small shrine in the middle of the forest. It has one large torii at the entrance and two smaller ones right in front of the shrine.

The trail continues through the forest and follows a little stream, till you get to a road again. You cross the railway lines and follow the road along the coast line for a short while. You cut through an area with houses and find a next temple with a beautiful garden (like at all temples) and Buddhist statues.

In this area some sign posts show you the way, till you get to the main road nr. 42. This is the busy coastal road from Shingu to Nachi. There is a pedestrian/cyclists pavement on which you can walk. On your left side you see the Ocean and some port activities, while on your right side you see a shopping area with some large stores and an enormous parking pace in front of it. There is also a MacDonald's and KFC, for those of you who have been craving for something other than rice, here would be the chance at getting something Western. At the end of this long stretch of stores and parking lot, you come to the Sano-oji remains. According to legends, it was a common practice for pilgrims to take a pebble from the beach in Sano, and carry it in the sleeve of their Yukata till reaching Kumano Nachi Taisha.

Here the pedestrian/cycling pavement basically ends and your only choice is to walk on the side of the road. The road is boxed in between the Ocean and cliffs, so there is no other way to walk. It is dangerous because the road has sharp curves and the approaching traffic doesn't see you till the last moment. You continue along road nr. 42 and even need to walk through a tunnel, named the Kogushi Tunnel with a length of 283 meters. Fortunately, there is a pedestrian pavement through the tunnel.

A bit further down the road there is another tunnel of 170 meters. The tour map, however, suggest that the Kumano Kodo path is not through the tunnel but over the hill above it. There are no clear signs on this path. There are some small signs in Japanese, but these are not the standard Kumano Kodo sign posts. Rather these little signs seem to have been made by locals. As I can't read them, I keep being uncertain if I am on the right path. The climb is steep but not long. I get many spider webs in my face and on my arms, and there are no other visible footprints from other hikers. It seems that if there are any other pilgrims taking this route along the coast, that they take the easier way through the tunnel. But as the die-hard pilgrim that I am, I of course take the Kumano Kodo way, where the rocks, boulders and pathway are overgrown and slippery from the moss.

Then for more than two kilometers there is no trail, no pedestrian path and you need to walk alongside the busy road nr. 42. You need to walk mostly in the gutter, as the road follows the coastline and the railway tracks. Only the last half kilometer it is possible to walk parallel to this road, on a small road surrounded by houses and fields.

This road leads straight to the Hamanomiya-oji and the Fudarakusan-ji. The Fudarakusan-ji has an interesting history. From the 9th till the 18th century, many of the head monks of this temple went out to sea in a small rudderless boat upon turning 60 years of age. You can see a replica of this boat in the small pavilion on the left side of the square in front of the temple. Local people would entrust their prayers for enlightenment to the monks, who would set out to sea without expecting to return. The monks sacrificed themselves for relieving other beings from suffering, which practice is called Fudarakutokai. Literally it means the belief of a suicidal boat journey in search for the Buddhist Pure Land. The Hamanomiya-oji is one of the 99 oji shrines along the Kumano Kodo. At this location the pilgrims used sea-water in the ritual of purification, the beach being only a few hundred meters from the Temple.

The stamps are in typical wooden stamp house on the left side of the pavilion containing the replica boat. There are two stamps to be obtained, one for the Temple (ji) and one for the Shrine (oji). These are respectively number 31 and 32. Not surprisingly, the stamp for the Temple shows a little boat.

From here it is just a 5-minute walk to Nachi-Station, where you can take either the bus or train back to your hotel.

This route did not feel like a pilgrimage but rather like an exploration. Route maps are only available in Japanese, none in English, because apparently there is not enough interest from foreign tourists to walk this stretch of the Kumano Kodo. And I can confirm that this is the case. During my four-hour hike of the 19 kilometers trail, I did not meet any other pilgrim, no Japanese nor any foreigner. So my best guess is that also the Japanese have limited interest in this route. There were only a limited number of signposts for guidance, and I was regularly wondering whether I was on the right trail. There have been several occasions where I wasn't, and had to walk back a few hundred meters to follow a different pathway.

From an environmental point of view this section of the route is not so interesting to walk, which is why most pilgrims take the train or bus from Shingu station to Nachi station. The only advantage of this section is that you don't need to carry any water or lunch package with you, as you come across ample opportunities for vending machines that provide drinks, and restaurants, including KFC and McDonalds.

This route gets a 3 out of 5 in the difficulty rating because of the difficulty of reading the route map, combined with inadequate sign postings at several locations and the dangerous path alongside the busy road. The walk itself is easy as about 90% is on the road, and only some small hills are climbed.

Highlight of this part: Feeling like an explorer, trying to read the Japanese map. The Kumano Kodo path on the rocky beach along the Pacific Ocean.

Low point of this part: the dangerous walk in the gutter of the busy road. Insufficient signposts leading to wrong turns and backtracking of small parts of the route.

Photos of the Section

Starting point Grand Shrine

Pavement signs

A look-alike the Grand Shrine

Grand Shrine look alike

Hama-oji

Hard path along the Pacific Ocean

With tsunami warning shields every 500 meters

The Kumano Kodo trail on the rocky beach

The right turn at the end of the beach

Bamboo forest trail

Koyazaka statues

Up the small hill

View on the Pacific Ocean

More moss overgrown trail

Another oji along the trail in the forest

Is this the path?

Road trail along the Ocean

Torii in front of the Oji next to a Temple

Temple statues   *An occasional signpost*

Along road nr. 42

Civilization?

Sano-oji remains

Dangerous

But no alternative route

Through this tunnel

Over this tunnel

The right trail over the tunnel?

Be careful

Hamanomiya-oji

Fudarakusan-ji Temple

Fudarakusan-ji Temple

Both stamps nr. 32 and 31

浜の宮王子・補陀洛山寺 押印所
Hamanomiya-oji & Fudarakusanji Temple Memorial Stamp

Fudarakutokai monument

Section 7: Fudarakusan-ji to Nachi Taisha Grand Shrine

Key Data

Walking distance:	ca. 8 km
Walking time:	ca. 2.5 to 3.5 hrs
Altitude meters:	ca. 550 meters
Lowest altitude:	ca. 10 meters
Highest altitude:	ca. 350 meters
Stamps at:	Ichinono-oji (30), Tafuke-oji (29), Hirou-jinja (28), Seiganto-ji (27), Kumano Nachi Taisha (26)
Markers:	none
Difficulty:	2 out of 5
Percentage of road:	ca. 70%

NAKAHECHI ROUTE		Altitude	0 km		Distance				Altitude
				5 km		10 km	15 km	20 km	
Section 7	Fudarakusan-ji to Nachi Taisha Grand Shrine	750							750
		500							500
		250							250
		0							0

30   29   28

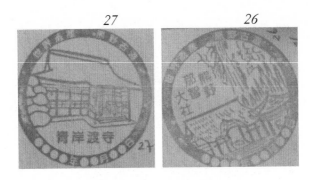

27   26

Description of the Section

The Fudarakusan-ji is only a few hundred meters from the Nachi bus and train station, which provide good and frequent connections to the town where you might have your accommodation, such as Shingu or Nachi-Katsuura. There are limited hotel accommodations in Nachisan. Neither Nachisan nor Shingu has accommodations with Onsen hot spring baths, unlike the location of Kii Katsuura which provides a large choice of accommodations and traditional Ryokans with hot springs. You can even select accommodations on a small Island, just off the Kii Katsuura port. I stayed in Hotel Nakanoshima, which is located on the small island, a five-minute hotel boat shuttle sail from the main marina of Kii Katsuura. It is a large accommodation offering the traditional Ryokan rooms and large indoor as well as outdoor hot spring baths. Having to get to your accommodation by ferry is a special experience.

Tip # 7: When visiting Nachi Taisha, stay at a Ryokan in Kii Katsuura, where you can enjoy the Onsen hot spring baths.

This route starts at the Fudarakusan-ji, from where the Kumano Kodo broadly follows the road nr. 43 and the Nachi River all the way up to the access point of the waterfall.

At the first small village the path turns away from the river and road nr. 43 and enters a forest. There are signposts which guide the way, but there are no markers for about a kilometer as the trail gently slopes up and then down again. The Japanese map (no English language map is available) is clear about the turns to take in the villages. The map actually shows a paved road, but in reality it is a trail through a dense forest of 10-meter tall bamboos (which is a grass) and trees. Towards the end of the forest trail there is an Oji on your right hand side, after which the path passes a cemetery before getting back to a small road running parallel to the main road nr. 43.

A kilometer later you pass the Ichinono-oji on your right hand side, where you obtain the first stamp on this route. It is stamp number 30.

The road continues to slope gently uphill between houses until it crosses the Nachi river, after which you see a large parking place and resting area along road nr. 43 on your left side. You cross this main road, and from here onwards you are not alone on the trail anymore, as you have arrived at the so called Daimon-zaka Slope, for which you first have to pass under a large torii and cross a small bridge.

From this point onwards the tourist numbers become crowds. Buses let off 40 tourists at a time, and large groups walk the final steps of the Kumano Kodo up to the Grand Shrine. During the first five kilometers I did not encounter any other tourist or pilgrim. It is pretty clear that all foreign and Japanese tourists take the public bus or their tour-bus, or even a taxi, to the Nachi Taisha Temple Complex. Nobody seems to walk the whole way up from Nachi town. Only a die-hard pilgrim would do that. Nachi Taisha has two main attractions: the Kumano Nachi Taisha Grand Shrine and Japan's highest waterfall. Both attractions draw thousands of tourists each day to this site. This is the busiest location of the Sanzan, which is already perceived at the foot of the Daimon-zaka Slope.

The stamp for the Tafuke-oji remains can be obtained at the little wooden stamp house that is in front of the store where you can rent traditional Japanese Kumano Kodo dress for photos shoots on this path. The stamp house is easily overlooked, so look for it on your left hand side, near the store entrance/window. The Tafuke-oji is the last Oji of the '99' from Kyoto, and also the last Oji of the Nakahechi Route. Historians assume that originally there was no Oji at this location, because this shrine was not mentioned in travel documents before the Edo period (from 1600). Presumably it was a final location, before accessing the Grand Shrine Complex, where nature and the impressive cedar trees were worshipped.

The Daimon-zaka Slope is the location where most of the marketing photos are taken, to be included in the many brochures about Kumano Kodo and Nachi Taisha. Often they will display a photo of two women in traditional red Kimono dress with the straw hat and white veil, hiking up the slope on their straw sandals. This costume originates from the Heian Period (800-1200), as worship attire worn by women. The path climbs over 300 stone steps, lined by impressive cedar trees. Two of these trees are thought to be 800 years old and have an enormous width. They are called Meoto-sugi, the 'husband and wife' cedar trees, standing left and right of the path.

Next you walk up a further 467 steps (I did not recount these or the earlier steps), along many tourist and souvenir shops, which gets you to the area of the Grand Shrine, at an elevation of ca. 350 meters above sea level. There are a number of interesting points and compared to the Grand Shrine complexes of Hayatama and Hongu Taisha, the complex here is very large, covering multiple levels and areas with buildings.

The Nachisan Seiganto-ji Temple is a wooden structure standing on poles and was built in 1590. You find your stamp number 27 on the right side of the Temple, in the usual little wooden house. The area in front of the Temple as well as inside the Temple is bustling with activities, as many Japanese tourists light incense in the large cauldron in front of the Temple, and pray inside the building (where shoes are left at the entrance of course). At none of the other Temples along the Nakahechi Route have I seen such interaction between the priests, monks, Buddhism and the pilgrims, as I observe here. I feel much more spiritually awakened by the open doors of the Temple, the incense burning in a big metal cauldron in front of the Temple, and the whole environment created by the buildings inside the Complex. This is a feeling which I did not have at any of the other locations and it feels good, despite being surrounded by the many other visitors and souvenir shops at the previous locations. The Seiganto-ji Temple was originally located close to the base of the Waterfall. According to local legends, in the 4th century, a holy Indian priest found a small image of Kannon when he was practicing nature worshipping and asceticism at the base of the Nachi Waterfall. It is the first temple of the 33-temple-pilgrimage (called Saigoku) in the Kansai area, which temples are dedicated to Kannon, serving protection and safeguarding for those worshipping, often dedicated to the travelers along the Kumano Kodo Routes.

The Kumano Nachi Taisha Grand Shrine is in the typical bright orange, and white colors, as also observed at the Hayatama Grand Shrine. Whereas at the Hayatama Grand Shrine the gate to access the square in front of the Shrine was open for all tourists and pilgrims, here at Nachi Taisha, the access gate is closed, and you can't get close. You can only peek at the Grand Shrine through the holes in the wooden fence. The Grand Shrine is a Shinto shrine, heading more than 4'000 Kumano shrines all over Japan. The religious origins are in the worship of nature, and at this location specifically Japan's highest waterfall, called the Nachi-no-Otaki. Stamp nr. 26 can be found on a small table on the left side of the shop selling religious articles. Although you can't get close to the Grand Shrine, on the main square of the Shrine Complex, there is also quite a large Shrine that is open to pilgrims. Also at this shrine, the interaction with pilgrims is much more present than at the other two Grand Shrines. From this perspective it is logical that many more tourists and pilgrims visit Nachi Taisha, compared to the other two Grand Shrines.

Close to the Shrine there is an enormous old tree that is hollow, and through which you can go. Belief has it that you first write your wish and name on a flat little wooden stick (for which you pay 300 Yen - $2.80), and then enter the small entrance of the tree, and inside the tree climb a 2-meter ladder to come out of the tree again, will make your wish come true. You place the stick in a rack next to the tree, from where presumable the monks take these prayer sticks for use in a burning ceremony, as could be observed during the Temple-Inn stay at Koyasan. But more about that in Chapter 7.

At the left side of the square in front of the Grand Shrine, you see high and broad wooden shelves with large cedar wooden barrels behind glass. These wooden barrels hold sake rice wine, given as offerings to the deities living in the Grand Shrine. The sake barrels are opened during ceremonies and the rice wine is shared between the participants and local people.

This area attracts the most tourists of all Kumano Kodo locations. And as usual, commerce has found its way to all those tourists as well. Compared to all other locations along the Kumano Kodo, at Nachi Taisha most commercial stores and souvenir shops can be found.

In order to get closer to the waterfall, you first walk down a road to get to the location of the pagoda. It is here where you can take the iconic photos of the waterfall together with the three story orange pagoda. You see that photo in all of the brochures for this area and the Kumano Kodo. This pagoda was reconstructed in 1972, more than 300 hundred years after the original pagoda was destroyed by fire.

You need to descend a lot of steps to get to a tour-bus parking place in the bend of the road. At this location there is a public toilet, some souvenir shops with small restaurants, as well as the Taki-mae bus stop, from where you can take the bus down to Nachi Station and Kii Katsuura. You need to cross the road and walk in between two tall cedar trees and through a large torii gate, to get down more steep steps in order to descend to the base of the waterfall. This stone step declining path is laid out for many tourists. It is very wide, has a handrail in the middle and on the right side, and is by far the broadest 'trail' of the Kumano Kodo, when not considering the roads. At the end of the many steps down, you arrive at the Hirou-jinja Shrine, comprising of a torii, an incense cauldron, wooden prayer sticks, and a religious souvenir shop. This Shrine worships the Nachi Waterfall, also called 'Ichi-no-taki' which is considered a diety itself, which is why the torii is at the end of the path, between you and the view on the waterfall. This is part of the worshipping of nature, where the waterfall is in focus of the Grand Shrine as well as the Temple. If you want to get closer to the waterfall, you need to buy a ticket for 300 Yen ($2.80) at the tourist shop on the left side. There you also find stamp nr. 28. This stamp is not in the usual little wooden house, but on a table, close to the touristic commercial and religious items. After the entrance gate you walk up steps for about a hundred meters till you get closer to the basin of the waterfall. As already mentioned before, this waterfall is Japan's highest, with a drop of 133 meters.

You need to walk back up the steep stone steps to get back to the Taki-mae bus stop. From there bus number 8 goes once or twice an hour (depending on the time of day) to Nachi Station and Kii Katsuura Station. You can easily sort out the bus time table via www.tb-kumano.jp or by asking the front office of your hotel.

In summary, this section of the Kumano Kodo is relatively short, only about three hours walking time. It is still a separate part, because you will need quite a lot of time to take in all the sights at the Nachi Taisha area. You can easily fill three hours from the Tafuke-oji at the beginning of the Daimon-zaka Slope, till you are finished at the waterfall. That means combined with the hike up from Nachi Station, it can be the better part of a day, particularly when you also include your traveling time to and from Nachi Station, depending on where your hotel is. Along the short hike itself there are no real service points, other than the occasional vending machine, but in Nachi Taisha there is everything you need. So for this section it is not necessary to carry liters of water or lunch boxes.

This route gets a 2 out of 5 in the difficulty rating because of the easy path, without strenuous ascents or descents, as about 70% is on the road and only some 550 meters in altitude are covered. Though the Daimon-zaka Slope is steep, it is rather short, as is the descent to the base of the Waterfall. You probably spend an equal amount of time sightseeing, as you do hiking.

Highlight of this part: The trail through the Bamboo forest at the start of this section. The Daimon-zaka Slope with its beautiful 800-year old cedar trees, where you can still observe women in their traditional red pilgrimage kimonos. The whole complex of the Grand Shrine and Temple at Nachi Taisha and the views on the mountains from there. The spirituality surrounding the Seiganto-ji temple. The view of the three story orange pagoda with Japans highest waterfall in the back. The primeval forest on your way to the base of the waterfall.

Low point of this part: After having experienced and enjoyed the solitude on many of the Kumano Kodo trails, the crowds of tourists at Nachi Taisha bring you back to commercial reality.

Photos of the Section

Follow the main road, and then the small parallel road

Also here trying to contain the river

Take the left trail   *through the forest*

Wooden bridges   *Bamboo forest*

Different types of under-footing

One of the few sign posts

Oji

Past the graveyard

Entrance to Ichinono-oji

Ichinono-oji

along the small road, across the Nachi River

Torii to the Daimon-zaka Slope

Tafuke-oji remains

Majestic cedar tree

800-year-old cedar trees

Posing between the Meoto-sugi

Not alone anymore

Steep up

Tourist shops along the climb   *Main gate*

Torii towards the Grand Shrine

Elaborate gardens

Distant views

Main hall of the Nachisan Seiganto-ji

Elevated floor　　　　*Very spiritual*

Nachi Taisha Grand Shrine

Front of grand Shrine

Stamp nr. 26 on the small table on the left

Small Shrine

Open for prayers   *Typical roofs*

Grand Shrine square

Sake barrels

Going in and getting out of the old tree

Tree with the place for the wishing sticks

Wide view

Close view

Parking and rest area before the gate to the Waterfall

Behind the bend in the street

Entrance and broad path down to the Waterfall

Entrance ticket and stamp on the left side

Hirou-jinja

Close to the base of the waterfall

The Nakanoshima hotel shuttle ferry coming from the Island

Traditional Ryokan room

Section 8: Kumano Nachi Taisha Grand Shrine to Koguchi

Key Data

Walking distance: ca. 15 km
Walking time: ca. 5 to 7 hrs
Altitude meters: ca. 1'960 meters
Lowest altitude: ca. 60 meters
Highest altitude: ca. 883 meters
Stamps at: Jizo-jaya Teahouse remains (25), Koguchi (24)
Markers: 1 to 29
Difficulty: 5 out of 5
Percentage of road: ca. 8%

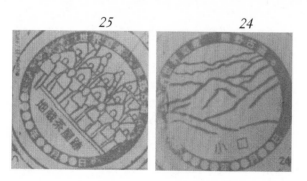

25   24

Description of the Section

Section 8 and Section 9 of this Chapter are 800-year-old "shortcuts" for the pilgrims to travel back to the Kumano Hongu Taisha Grand Shrine, on their way back to Kyoto. Instead of taking the long way back, by walking to the Hayatama Grand Shrine and then by boat to Hongu Taisha, a more direct route was found. The travel route back the way they came would have been with little efforts and hardship, but much more time. The short cut route via Koguchi, however, goes over the mountains and is rather difficult. It shortened the distance from around 60 kilometers by 50%, to around 30 kilometers, and would enable a safe return in case the river level and rapids would carry too much water to take the flat-bottom boat back up against stream.

The route from the Nachi Taisha Grand Shrine to Koguchi is generally considered the most arduous part of the Nakahechi route and is called the 'Ogumotori-goe' section. This means 'passing over clouds', because of the altitude of the two passes. It reaches the highest elevation of ca. 883 meters above sea level, within ca. 5 kilometers after your start at Kumano Nachi Taisha Grand Shrine, which is at ca. 350 meters. You can add another 100 meters if you start at the waterfall. Not many people walk this route. During my hike, I met a handful of other hikers, plus one tour group with a guide. Almost all of them walked from Koguchi to Nachi Taisha, so the opposite direction. The people I met were either Japanese, American or French. If you are seeking solitude as a pilgrim, then this trail is ideal. It seems to be too heavy or inconvenient for most easy going hikers to walk.

The route is completely through the forest without coming across any villages or other modern service points. Only right after the beginning or right before the end you have one possibility to get drinking water, so carry sufficient water with you. You will also need a lunch box from your hotel.

After one kilometer of walking up steep stone steps through the forest you arrive at the Nachi Kogen Highland Park. During your climb to this point, you could still hear the waterfall in the far distance. The Nachi Kogen Highland Park is an open area, with blossom trees lined along grass fields, and several entertainment areas such as a long metal slide. You walk up the steep hill on the right side of the entertainment grounds, till you reach the parking lot at the top. There you take a right turn and walk a few hundred meters over the asphalt road till you get to the trailhead at the end of the unpaved parking lot. The trail starts with stone steps, which changes to soft forest soil at occasions, but often the path has uneven rocks, so that you need to watch where you put your feet. For a long time, the trail is parallel to the mountain road, sometimes close, sometimes further away.

The first climb to the Funami-toge pass at ca. 883 meters is relatively steep, and there are many steps to be conquered going up. It may not seem much to cover the ca. 533 altitude difference within ca. 5 kilometers, but this section also includes some horizontal pathways, or even some slightly descending. So a lot of the climb is concentrated on a number of longer steep stretches. What makes it extra difficult are the stone steps that go on and on, though regularly separated by soil paths. The difficulty about the stone steps is that they are extremely uneven.

At the first half of the trail, the half kilometer markers are different from those on all other trails. The markers here are small stones instead of the taller wood-like pillars. The distance markers start at 1 at Nachi Taisha and end with 29 in Koguchi.

Shortly before the Funami-toge pass, you came across the Funami-jaya Teahouse remains between distance markers 8 and 9. At this location there is a really good viewpoint just 50 meters off the trail, worthwhile to visit. It provides a wide panoramic view on the Nachi Kogen Park and Nachi-Katsuura city and you can see the Pacific Ocean. For about two kilometers the trail stays around the altitude of around 800 meters, until it descends to ca. 700 meters. Not that you can relax your leg muscles during that descent. It involves more stone steps, and balancing your feet on the uneven stones is extremely exhausting for your knees. That is at least until you get to the same road, to which the trail was running parallel during the first ca. 7 kilometers. The road gently descends for about a kilometer which is a relieve for the legs and knees. You walk parallel to a little stream with crystal clear mountain water. Before the road turns into the forest trail again, you come across the Jizo-jaya Teahouse remains. It is at this location where you collect your stamp number 24, the first stamp of the day.

As soon as you change from the road to the trail, it goes up again to the second pass at around 805 meters, called the Ishikura-toge pass. The going up and down continues, and for a further kilometer you ascend to ca. 870 meters, the Echizen-toge pass. Together with the Funami-toge pass at 883 meters, this is the highest point on the Nakahechi Route. This pass is in the middle of the forest, so there is no viewpoint. During the day, almost mid-April, it was very windy, and the wind was cold. As with all mountains, the weather can quickly change, so be sure you bring sufficient warm clothing.

Tip # 8: Depending on the time of year of your hike, the wind, coming from the Ocean through the main valley, can be cold. So bring a warm jacket or sweater.

The pass is followed by an extremely steep descent via uneven stone steps. These steps bring you from ca. 870 meters to ca. 340 meters above sea level within ca. 2.4 kilometer. This descent is almost double the steepness of the ascent to the first pass. Prepare your knees for a battering! This is one of the reasons why most pilgrims and hikers actually walk the Ogumotori-goe section from Koguchi to Nachi Taisha, so in opposite direction. Your knees might thank you for such decision.

Along the trail you pass several small jizo statues as well as monuments with poems on them. About 2.5 kilometers before Koguchi you pass the Kusu-no-Kubo Lodging remains. According to history, there were over 10 traveler lodgings (Hatago's) along a 1.5 kilometers stretch known as the Kusu-no-Kubo. These Hatago's were operated until the early 20st century, the last ones remaining after a long history along the Kumano Kodo Routes.

Uneven steps of moss-covered rocks keep changing with soft forest dirt under-footing. The rock steps keep making the descent heavy and difficult, particularly after the extremely long and steep rocky descent from earlier in the day. About one kilometer before the end of the trail, you pass the Waroda-ishi Rock. This is a moss covered large boulder that has three symbols carved in 'Bonji' (I refer to Section 4 in this Chapter, where Bonji was already explained). The three symbols are: Kannon, the Bodhisattva of safety and relieve of suffering as worshipped at Nachi Taisha, Yakushi, the medicine Buddha of Healing, as worshipped at Hayatama Taisha, and Amida, the Buddha of Compassion and Wisdom, as worshipped at Hongu Taisha. According to local legend, these three Kumano deities would meet at this boulder and chat over tea.

Shortly before the end of the trail you can see the road and the koguchi-gawa River and the results of deforestation and landslides to your right side, eating deep into the mountains. Not a pretty sight. Right at the end of the forest trail is where you collect your stamp number 23. The little stamp house is at the left side of the trail, just before descending the final steps to the road.

Getting a bus in or out of Koguchi can be quite time consuming. Depending on where you are staying (Hongu Taisha, Shingu or Kii Katsuura), a bus trip itself could take up to two hours, including transfer time (in case of Kii Katsuura). The bus service from Koguchi to Shingu or Hong Taisha is extremely irregular. If you are unlucky with (the planning of) the ending time of your hike, you could end up waiting for a long time till a public bus collects you. I am talking about hours. This is one more reason why many pilgrims walk the Ogumotori-goe route with a start in Koguchi. The buses from Nachi Taisha to Shingu or Kii Katsuura are much more frequent, because of the large number of tourists there. When you hike later in the day and plan an arrival in Koguchi late afternoon or evening, you run a risk of getting stuck there. There are three accommodations in Koguchi, but you need to reserve well in advance via the Kumano-Travel System in order to get a place for the night. So it is advisable to sort out the timing of the buses through www.tb-kumano.jp or with the help of the front desk of your hotel.

As the trail is heavy on the legs, you may think about staying at an Onsen during the night, so that the healing powers of the natural minerals of the hot springs would enable your strained legs and muscles to recover. As Koguchi does not have an Onsen, you would need to select another location, such as Kawayu Onsen or Kii Katsuura. The hiking time together with the commuting time by bus, probably makes this a relatively long day.

Tip # 5: Plan your arrival in Koguchi in such a way that you have a good chance of catching the public bus, without having to wait for hours. Sort out the bus time tables in advance, either via the Internet or at the local Tourist Information Center. In case you want to spend the night at one of the three accommodations in the village, make sure that you make your reservation well in advance.

This route gets a 5 out of 5 in the difficulty rating because it has three passes above 800 meters and covers a high number of altitude meters in a relative short trek. Particularly the long stretches of moss covered and uneven extremely steep passages of ascent as well as descent make this a very arduous trail to walk.

Highlight of this part: The feeling of solitude on the trail after the tourist crowds of Nachi Taisha. The beautiful primeval forests.

Low point of this part: The strain on your knees during and at the end of the hike, caused by the very long and steep stone covered descent.

Photos of the Section

Different distance markers

Steep up

Nachi Kogen Highland Park

Spring colors in the park

Signpost

Across the parking lot

Steep up

And up

Road never far away

Horizontal   *And up*

View on the Ocean and Katsuura

Funami-toge pass at ca. 883 meters

Down to the right

Difficult trails

Difficult trail   *Easy trail*

Jizo-jaya Teahouse remains – resting area and stamp nr. 24

Steep up

Jizo

More up, along Jizo and poem monument

In the middle of the forest

More up

People put the trail in right perspective

Ishikura-toge pass at ca. 805 meters

Steep down   *The hiker puts the trail in size perspective*

Easy down trail

Tranquility

Kusu-no-Kubo Lodging remains

Steep down   *Easy down*

Uneven and slippery

Waroda-ishi Rock

Last steep and slippery steps down

End of trail in Koguchi, with stamp house on top of stairs, to the right

Koguchi Village

Bus stop

Section 9: Koguchi to Ukegawa

Key Data

Walking distance:	ca. 14.5 km
Walking time:	ca. 4 to 6 hrs
Altitude meters:	ca. 1'050 meters
Lowest altitude:	ca. 60 meters
Highest altitude:	ca. 460 meters
Stamps at:	Kowase Ferry Remains (23), Ishido-jaya Teahouse remains (22), Ukegawa (21)
Markers:	29 to 54
Difficulty:	3 out of 5
Percentage of road:	ca. 9%

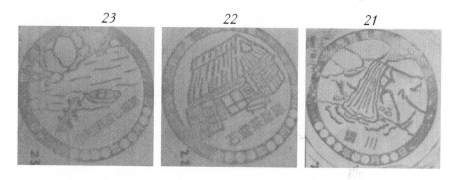

Description of the Section

Getting to Koguchi to start your day hike to Ukegawa is not easy and may involve one to two hours of bus travel. I refer to my explanations at the end of the previous Section 8 in this Chapter.

In case you walked the Ogumotori-goe section from Kumano Nachi Taisha the day before, you will already have obtained stamp number 24. In case you haven't and are looking for the stamp at Koguchi: it is at the end of the trail coming from Nachi Taisha, which is not too far away from the Koguchi bus stop and which trail's end is signposted on the road.

On a little side road, down from the main road number 44, you find a little shrine and a few small buildings plus a rest area, however without any explanation signs in the English language. The shrine is next to the Koguchi Shizen-no-le Lodging, which is an old junior high school that was turned into a lodging accommodation.

From the bus stop you need to walk along the main road number 44 (without a pedestrian path, so be careful of the cars) towards the North (away from the Ogumotori-goe trail end). After about 500 meters you need to make a choice. The asphalt road continues through a tunnel, but the original Kumano Kodo path goes over the hill of the tunnel. Of course I take the trail over the hill, which way is signposted, as 800 years ago there was no tunnel either.

Apparently nobody takes this forest trail over the hill, because a large part of the path is extremely covered with moss and grass, and there are many spider webs across the trail. The trial goes up pretty steep, mostly on stone steps and the same down again. You pass two locations with small Jizo statues, and at the end the path goes along a small graveyard till you get to the Akagi-gawa River, a small stream in a broad rocky riverbed. You pass another small Jizo statue wearing a bib, while you walk on a small hardened path with the river on your left side and houses on your right side, till you arrive at the Kowase ferry remains. At this location there is a parking place and a rest area, as well as the stamp house, where you can obtain stamp number 23 for your booklet. For many hikers this location is the starting point of their day walk on the Kogumotori-goe section, as evidenced by the parking lot, the road sign post, and a collection of wooden and bamboo walking canes that can be taken for use on the trail.

You cross the Kowase-bashi Bridge at this location, and after some signposted turns, you start your climb up steep steps soon exchanged for uneven moss covered rocks. You pass the Okiri Jizo statue on your left side, and continue up the mountain. During about 2.5 kilometers the trail rises ca. 300 meters, on different kinds of under-footing, such as soft forest dirt, big uneven rocks, steep stone steps and a dirt path covered with small lose stones. Along the way you have nice views to the Akagi-gawa river valley and you pass several monuments with poems on them, which are about one and a half meter tall stone poles with Kanji inscriptions. The forest is peaceful and quiet, and since the path follows the side of the mountain, the sun regularly shines in on you. At the Sakura-chaya teahouse remains there is an information table and two benches, but other than that, there is nothing left from the remains. As usual, you see just a flattened empty plot of land. The teahouse was named after a large cherry tree (hence the name Sakura), and this location was used for a teahouse until the early 20th century.

About half a kilometer later, after a continued climb on a relative easy path, you arrive at the highest point of this section, the Sakura-toge pass at ca. 460 meters of altitude. The pass level is marked by distance marker number 36, as well as a poem monument. Since the pass is in the middle of the forest, there is no viewpoint.

After the pass, the trail goes down steeply for a short distance, after which the trails becomes more or less level with an easy under-footing. The trail slowly descends to an altitude of around 400 meters when you reach the Ishido-jaya teahouse remains. The name is derived from the whetstones (used to sharpen metal) that were found in the area and the teahouse was mentioned in travel dairies from the Edo era (from 1600). According to historical documents, multiple travel Inns (Hatago) and Teahouses stood at this location, which makes sense, because it is about half way the Kogumotori-goe section. As usual, nothing remains, and you only see a covered resting area, a poem monument and the little stamp house for stamp number 22.

Close to distance marker number 40 you pass the Sai-no-kawara Jizo statue on your right hand side. It is a small stone statue with a big pile of rocks in front of it. The pile of rocks has an interesting story to it. The Jizo is a Bodhisattva, protector of children and travelers, and in this case protects young children that did not accumulate enough Karma to pass the river that divides this world from the after world. The stacking of pebbles represents the prayers of the young children for their soul to find peace, or to console the souls of pilgrims who lost their life during the Kumano Kodo.

The trail continues with sloping up and down, but remains relatively easy. From the point where you cross an asphalt road, however, the trail ascends again to an elevation of ca. 460 meters when you reach the Hyakken-gura Lookout point. You can enjoy a wide view over the many green mountains. A small Jizo accompanies the view.

From here you basically have a 5.5 kilometers long descent to Ukegawa. The first part of the descent is rather steep, while you pass another small Jizo wearing a faded bib, and come passed the junction with the Iseji Route, close to distance marker 46. Shortly before marker 47 you pass the Matsuhata Teahouse remains, showing an overgrown flat area. The remainder of the descent is very gradual on an easy path of mostly forest dirt and leaves. The end of the trail runs between several houses and after several turns you arrive at the main street number 168. Right there is where you find the little stamp house with number 21 for Ukegawa. Don't forget to stamp your booklet, before you dash off to the bus stop or to walk the remainder on the road to your accommodation.

Ukegawa is close to Kawayu Onsen, which is only a 25-minute walk from the end of the trail. I advise you to enjoy a hotel accommodation in one of the three Onsen (Kawayu, Wataze or Yunomine), in order to enjoy the hot spring bath after your day hiking.

Tip # 16: Consider booking your accommodation in one of the Onsen close by (Kawayu, Wataze or Yunomine), so that you can relax in a hot spring bath after completing your day hike.

There are no service points on this trail. After you leave the Kowase Ferry remains, you are on your own. There are no drinking water taps, drinks vending machines or kiosks offering food. So make sure that you are foreseen with sufficient water and a lunch packet. Like on all trails of the Kumano Kodo, there are no bins along the routes and you need to carry all your trash with you till you reach your hotel.

This route gets a 3 out of 5 in the difficulty rating because the distance is relatively short and the number of altitude meters is relatively low, when compared to some other sections of the Nakahechi Route. According to many people this section is the second-most difficult, after the Ogumotori-goe section, but I disagree with that opinion. Have a closer look at the comparison of my difficulty ratings and trail charts and statistics at the beginning of this Chapter.

This route is completely through the forests. Apart from a bit of asphalt road in the village of Koguchi, when walking from the bus stop to the start of the forest trail, all is unpaved track. Not many people traverse this section of the Nakahechi Route. During my trek I met only a few people, a lot less than on the routes between Takijiri-oji and Hongu Taisha. This latter route seems to be very popular, particularly for travelers that only want to hike a short section of the trail. Because of the few travelers on the path, there were many sections where the stones and rock steps were overgrown with moss. The many ferns and moss, like on the previous trails, show how humid this habitat is. The limited number of hikers left insufficient footprints on the moss covered rocks and steps, making them extremely slippery at some spots.

Highlight of this part: Viewpoint at Hyakken-gura. Solitude in the beautiful forests.

Low point of this part: Slippery stones and many steps. The middle of the trail is a continuous up and down.

Photos of the Section

Local shrine in Koguchi

You came from there

Trail over the tunnel

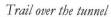

Along small Jizo statues

Past the graveyard

Along the Akagi-gawa River

Small Jizo

Stamp house at Kowase-bashi Bridge

View back to the bridge

Steep up with nice views

Mystic

Okiri Jizo

Difficult under-footing

Panoramic views

Sakura-chaya teahouse remains

At the Sakura-toge pass, ca. 460 meters   *Monument*

Easy pathways

Ishido-jaya teahouse remains with stamp nr. 22

Sai-no-kawara Jizo statue

Sai-no-kawara Jizo statue

Easy descent

Also up again

Hyakken-gura lookout point at ca. 460 meters

Countless mountain tops

Matsuhata Teahouse remains

Easy pathway

Arriving at Ukegawa

Chapter 7

THE KOHECHI ROUTE

Getting to Koyasan

Koyasan is the starting point of the Kumano Kodo Kohechi Route. Koyasan is located on a plateau in the Kii mountains at an elevation of ca. 900 meters, and stretches out over about six kilometers West to East and about three kilometers North to South.

Wherever you are coming from (Kyoto, Osaka, Kobe, Nagoya or Tokyo), most public transport to Koyasan converges at the Hashimoto train station (Prefecture Wakayama). From there only one train, the Nankai Koya Line Express, snakes into the mountains for about 45 minutes to the Gokurakubashi train station (440 Yen, $3.95). From this station a cable car is pulled up a steep stretch of mountain, and arrives in Koyasan in five minutes (390 Yen, $3.50). The cable car covers an altitude difference of ca. 330 meters, from ca. 539 to ca. 869 meters above sea level. At the cable car station in Koyasan, three bus lines bring the tourists to each of their destinations in the Temple town, which is further uphill. It costs 290 Yen ($2.60) for six bus stops on Line 2 to reach the Koyasan Tourist Office.

From above description it may seem that Koyasan can be reached easily and in little time. This might be deceptive, depending on where you are coming from. For example, I was coming from Kii Katsuura, at the South tip of the Kii Peninsula, having completed the Nakahechi Route. I had the

6:48 a.m. train from there, which brought me to Wakayama station in almost 3 hours. There I had only two minutes to catch a connecting train to Hashimoto (Wakayama Prefecture). Because of the change from platform 1 to 7, I missed this train by about five seconds, which meant that I had to wait an hour for the next train. That was not so bad, because it gave me a chance to have a late breakfast at the coffee shop at the station. Generally, the hotels only start breakfast at 7 a.m., and as I had to leave before that time without a filled stomach, the opportunity for a late breakfast was appreciated. After a week of having a lot of rice and green tea for breakfast, it was also nice to have some other type of food again, cappuccino and filled sandwiches.

The next train took me to Hashimoto station in little over an hour. Not that it was that far, but because the train stopped everywhere, like a bus, stopping at every small station. Another resemblance with the bus was that at these small locations, where there was no ticket machine or ticket office, the local commuters paid the train driver, depending on the number of stations they travelled, at disembarking. The front wagon had the same display as in the bus, showing increasing fare amounts as stations passed. Arriving at Hashimoto I had to buy another ticket, since the track till Hashimoto was run by Japan Rail (JR West), whereas the final track to Koyasan was run by the Nankai Koya Line. At the train station in Kii Katsuura, I could not buy one ticket for the whole route, so I bought one ticket for JR, and at Hashimoto had to buy my second ticket for the Nankai Koya Line. At Hashimoto I had 13 minutes transfer time, which was sufficient.

At Gokurakubashi I had a five-minute transfer time, which was also sufficient. At this last station basically all travelers from the Nankai train moved in one large procession to the cable car, all wanting to get to Koyasan. It took me a little over six hours altogether to get there, from 6:48 a.m. till 1:08 p.m.

When you are close to Kii Tanabe, there is an alternative way to get to Koyasan. There is a bus connection from there to Koyasan, which also takes about six hours, including transfer at Ryujin Onsen. In case you want to explore this option, coordinate with the front desk of your hotel or with the Tourist Information Office in Hongu, Tanabe, or other place that you are staying. I was warned that this bus connection is not always 100%

reliable, and for example between Ryujin Onsen and Koyasan the bus does not run in the winter or during weekdays for certain months of the year.

Tip # 11: In case you are not close to Koyasan, sort out your train or bus time tables. HyperDia (www.Hyperdia.com) is good for planning your train trip, costs and times. You might have to allocate a day to get to Koyasan.

Slow train like a bus *Nankai Koya Line*

Cable car

Koyasan

Koyasan is a small town having a large number of Temples, Shukubo (Temple-Inns) and a number of tourist shops, convenience stores and some houses, and even has schools and a hospital. Koyasan was founded in the year 816 by a Buddhist monk called Kobo Daishi, who wanted to have a Buddhist retreat deep in the mountains. The temples focus on Buddhist practices and studies, following the Shingon Buddhism. For more than a thousand years, people made their pilgrimage to Koyasan to experience this small and isolated Buddhist mountain retreat, which had almost 2'000 temples up to two hundred years ago. During the recent ages most of the temples were destroyed by fires, and many of them were combined, so that at present there are approximately 120 temples left, of which 52 provide lodgings.

In July 2004, Koyasan was registered as a UNESCO World Heritage Site, as part of the "Sacred Sites and Pilgrimage Routes in the Kii Mountain Range, and the cultural landscapes that surround them".

For three main reasons you should visit the Koyasan Tourist Office on your day of arrival. First, you need to obtain your first stamp there (number 37). The Tourist Office stamp is the first stamp of the route: it is on the left side in their store, just ask for it. Second, the Kohechi Route has a special stamp booklet, though in Japanese only. Have the friendly ladies at the Tourist Office explain the locations of the stamps for the Japanese booklet, as each of the six stamps has a pre-allocated space on the page. I used this special booklet in addition to the regular dual pilgrimage booklet for collecting the stamps on this route. Third, the Tourist Office has good sightseeing maps of Koyasan, indicating the main temples, locations of the Shukubos, etc.

Tip # 12: Visit the Tourist Office in Koyasan to obtain your first stamp, the special Kohechi stamp booklet and local sightseeing brochures.

You should plan for sightseeing in Koyasan. I arrived there around 1:30 p.m., and could not check-in to my Shukubo till after 3 p.m., so I went sightseeing for the afternoon. Koyasan is so small that you can easily walk to all the sights and then back to your Shukubo. There are many sights to be seen, and the top three attractions are the Kongobu-ji, the Danjo Garan Complex, and the Okuno-in.

The Kongobu-ji is the head Temple for the Koyasan Shingon Buddhism, overseeing some 3'600 temples all over Japan, and is open for tourists against an admission fee of 500 Yen ($4.60) You will see old and beautiful screen paintings (of which it is not allowed to take photos) on the sliding doors (called fusuma), and the Banryutei, Japan's largest rock garden with wave patterns designed in the small white rocks. As in all temples and Shukubo, you don't wear shoes inside the building. At the entrance of the building you can store your shoes in a rack and put on a pair of the one-size-fit-all slippers. You are likely to frequently lose one or both of the slippers, for example when ascending or descending stairs, because of their large sizes and slippery plastic material. The wooden walkways, tatami rooms and screens breathe an atmosphere of old age and tranquility. It feels very special walking through the Kongobu-ji temple, one of the few where you can actually enter. Because this building is the administrative head-office, there are only few statues to see during the tour. At the ticket office you can buy beautiful handmade calligraphy combined with red temple stamps.

The Danjo Garan Complex has four main temples, historically used as a quiet and secluded place for the training of Buddhist monks. It has a great two story Pagoda, called Konpon Daito, which interior is beautifully decorated. At its center it has a statue of Buddha Mahavairochana, which is surrounded by four Buddhas, with sixteen bodhisattvas painted on the surrounding pillars. The design is a three dimensional expression of the mandalas of Shingon Buddhism.

The second main Temple is the Kondo, or Golden Hall, where the major Buddhist ceremonies are performed, and which holds a large Buddha statue.

The third main structure is the Fudodo, being the oldest building in Koyasan, originating from 1197, and having escaped the many fires in the area over the ages. As this is an original building, it was named National Treasure. There is no access to this building.

The fourth main building in the complex is called Mie-do, or Portrait Hall. This is supposed to be the place where Kobo Daishi had his residence, and this building is opened only one day in the year, an evening in March when Kobo Daishi is believed to have entered into eternal mediation in the year 835.
In none of these buildings is it allowed to make photos inside.

The Okuno-in is a graveyard containing more than 200'000 grave stones and monuments along a narrow path, stretching for about 2.5 kilometers. Many local famous people are interred there, and at the end of the path is the Okuno-in, a mausoleum for Kobo Daishi, where he is said to be in eternal meditation for the liberation of all beings.

Tip # 13: Plan to have at least a full day of sightseeing in Koyasan, as there are many interesting Buddhist buildings and historical places to experience.

Koyasan has four distinct seasons, and the spring season is probably the most beautiful, when the cherry blossoms (sakura) bloom from mid-April and the rhododendrons (shakunage) bloom from beginning of May. They bloom later than in other parts of Japan because of the elevation of Koyasan.

Tip # 14: Plan your visit to Koyasan in Spring time, ideally April or May.

Koyasan has 52 Temple lodgings called Shukubo. There is no other type of hotel or "normal" hotel. The stay in the Temple-inn is an extraordinary experience that should not be missed. The Temple-inn is run by monks and provides accommodation, dinner and breakfast for the overnight guests. Like at the traditional Japanese Ryokans, all rooms have tatami mats and sliding doors. The sliding doors have no locks, but the room has a small safe for valuables.

The table in your room is low, and there are no chairs, as you sit on a cushion with crossed legs or your legs under the low table. The check-in office is like that as well. Several monks do the administration, sitting behind the low tables surrounded by binders and paperwork, but also have a laptop in front of them. Most tourists travel in groups and share a room per group. That means that in one room multiple futon mats are placed next to each other, covered with a thick blanket against the cold. Each room does have a heater, and the low table has an electrically heated blanket underneath, with which you can cover your folded legs. Dinner and breakfast are typically served in the room, except when you are a single traveler, or a couple, then breakfast is in a common room. The meals are Buddhist vegetarian, called Shojin Ryori, and include a soup dish, a grilled dish, a pickled dish, a deep fried dish, and a tofu dish.

I am staying at Muryoko-inn Temple which has the typical common bathroom, separated for men and women. The bathroom has the low plastic seats and the water tap low at the wall, and may only be used till 9 p.m., after which it closes and can't be used in the morning. The toilets at that bathroom include the old squat type toilets, however, there are also other modern toilets closer to the guest rooms. These toilets are new, and even have the seat heating and bottom-washing water spray. As in all Ryokans, you don't wear your shoes inside but you wear house slippers, in the one-size-fit-all, which means that they frequently slip off your feet when ascending or descending the stairs. In the bathroom these house slippers are exchanged for toilet room slippers. Apart from a modern toilet, it also has a wash room, where you can wash your face, hands and upper body. All guests share these bathroom and toilet facilities. The guest rooms have no TV, but perhaps the monks do. Wi-Fi is everywhere in the temple, and there is a good connection in the guestrooms.

The whole building is made of wood, with some walls made of clay. It has a beautiful courtyard garden to promote tranquility for the mind.

The highlight of the stay at the Temple-inn is the attendance of the morning prayers and meditation of the Monks. The prayer room is divided in two parts; one part for the tourists with more than 50 small seats, and the other part where the monks have their shrines, statues and perform the prayers. Shortly before 6 p.m., as well as 6 a.m., a monk sounds a gong several times to call all monks for prayer. The morning ceremony can be watched by the tourists. It is very special to hear the chanting, accompanied by the ringing of a bell and a gong for almost an hour and a half. The room is lit by several candles and to the right side a monk keeps a fire burning with small pieces of wood. In each guest room, as well as in the ante-room to the meditation room, there are long flat wooden sticks (called Ema) on which you can write your name and prayer or wish. You pay a small amount for having such wish-sticks used in prayers and burned in the fire. The dimmed light, candles, incense and chanting of the monks brings a special mystique to the room. After 40 minutes, one of the 12 monk comes to ask the watching guests to follow him, and he guides them in a row through the prayer area, while the monks keep chanting. You get a good close up of the religious objects in the area. The ceremony ends at 7:30 a.m. and breakfast is served from 8 a.m., after which most tour groups and travelers check out.

Tip # 15: Get up early to attend the Buddhist morning prayer and meditation session from 6 till 7:30 a.m.

Blossoms in Koyasan

Danjo Garan Temple Complex

Danjo Garan Entrance Gate

Entrance to Kongobu-ji

Hans Beumer

Kongobu-ji

Banryutei

273

Ceremony and Tea Room

Wooden floors and sliding doors

And no foot prints

Konpon Daito

Konpon Daito

Kondo

Fudodo

Mie-do

Muryoko-inn Temple Entrance gate

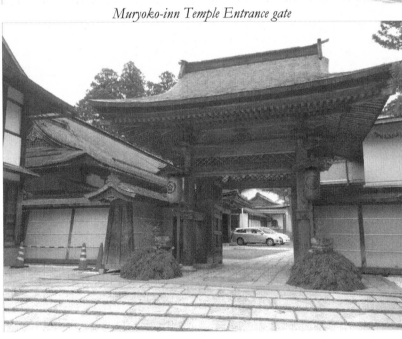

Muryoko-inn Temple Check-in

Room at the Temple-inn

Dinner served in the ante-room

Hallway

Monk gonging for evening prayers

Shared washing basin

Courtyard garden

Morning ceremony

Summary of the 4 Kohechi Sections

The Kohechi Route starts in Koyasan and finishes in Hongu Taisha, with a length of ca. 73 kilometers. This route provides a direct access from the area north of Koyasan, such as Nara, to the Kumano Sanzan region, and was a most frequently traversed pilgrimage route until the 17th century.

The mountain town at an elevation of around 900 meters is an excellent starting point for the Kohechi Route. The trails take you over four mountain passes, ranging between 1'000 and 1'250 meters in altitude. There are good and detailed route maps for the four days of this hike, which can be obtained at the Kumano Tourist Offices or online at www.tb-kumano.jp. Accommodations along the route can be easily booked via the Kumano Travel Reservation System (www.kumano-travel.com).

Key statistics for the Kohechi Route are as follows:

KOHECHI ROUTE (all numbers are estimates based on personal experience)	Section 1 Koyasan to Omata	Section 2 Omata to Miura-guchi	Section 3 Miura-guchi to Totsukawa	Section 4 Totsukawa to Hongu Taisha Grand Shrine	Total
Walking distance (km)	18.5	16.2	20.1	18.5	73.3
Walking time (hrs)	4 to 6	4 to 6	5 to 7	5 to 7	18 to 26
Altitude meters	1'400	2'040	1'900	2'300	7'640
Lowest altitude (meters)	670	333	160	90	
Highest altitude (meters)	1'200	1'245	1'080	1'060	
Stamps	37-38	39	40	41 +18	6
Difficulty	3 out of 5	5 out of 5	4 out of 5	5 out of 5	4.3 out of 5
Percentage of road	65%	5%	38%	14%	31%

The following chart shows the length and altitudes, enabling a better comparison of the four Sections.

KOHECHI ROUTE					Distance					
(all numbers are estimates based on personal experience)		Altitude	0 km	5 km	10 km	15 km	20 km	Altitude
Section 1	Koyasan to Omata	1'250 1'000 750 500 250 0						1'250 1'000 750 500 250 0
Section 2	Omata to Miura-guchi	1'250 1'000 750 500 250 0						1'250 1'000 750 500 250 0
Section 3	Miura-guchi to Totsukawa	1'250 1'000 750 500 250 0						1'250 1'000 750 500 250 0
Section 4	Totsukawa to Hongu Taisha Grand Shrine	1'250 1'000 750 500 250 0						1'250 1'000 750 500 250 0

Kohechi Route Stamp Booklet (in Japanese)

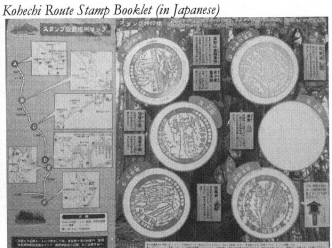

Section 1: Koyasan to Omata

Key Data

Distance:	ca. 18.5 km
Duration:	ca. 4 to 6 hrs.
Altitude meters:	ca. 1'400 meters
Lowest altitude:	ca. 670 meters
Highest altitude:	ca. 1'200 meters
Stamps at:	Koyasan Tourist Office (37), Your hotel at Omata, (38).
Difficulty:	3 out of 5
Percentage of road:	ca. 65%

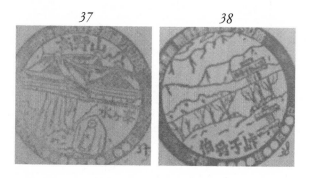

37   38

Description of the Section

The Shukubo doesn't provide a lunch box, so you will need to get one, or some snacks for underway, from one of the convenience stores in Koyasan.

Don't forget your first stamp at the Koyasan Tourist Office before you depart on the trail. It is easy to walk to the Kumano Kodo trail head, which starts just a few minutes' walk from the Tourist Office. There is no need to take a bus. The trail starts with a narrow concrete road that takes you quite steep uphill for about the first kilometer.

When you arrive at the Otaki-guchi Nyonin-do site, there is a little wooden house with a stamp in it. This is, however, not a formal Kumano Kodo stamp, as it is not formally listed, and this stamp has black ink; all Kumano Kodo stamps have red ink. When you want to collect this stamp, make sure that you have enough space in your stamp booklet. I carried four stamp books. A stamp book has space for 30 stamps, and the complete Nakahechi route already requires 36 stamps. So I used two for the Nakahechi route, one for Kohechi Route. I place the black stamp at the end of my Kohechi Route stamp booklet, to separate them from the official stamps.

Tip # 16: Carry four stamp booklets to collect all your stamps when hiking the Nakahechi and the Kohechi Routes.

The Otaki-guchi Nyonin-do site is a special site. Nyonin-do means women's temple, of which there were seven, one at each of the seven entrances to Koyasan. Those women's temples originate from the times during which women were not allowed to access Koyasan. At the present site, nothing remains to be seen from this temple, only this memorial stamp.

Call # 4: The local black stamp seems to be created by the local village. It would be better to have all stamps along the route coordinated with the Koyasan Tourist Office and made part of the official Kumano Kodo stamps.

The trail continues on the concrete small road and goes up only slightly for the next several kilometers. It is a relatively easy walk with wide panoramic views on the green mountains close by and in the distance. Without much effort you reach the Susuki-toge pass at almost 1'100 meters in altitude. At that point the path leads you to an unpaved forest trail, and finally you are feeling the leaves, branches, moss and tree roots below the soles of your hiking shoes again. That walks so much better than the concrete potholed road. At the pass level the path takes a turn and you descend at the other side of the mountain. The descent is rather steep, but gentle on the knees (when compared to the descent on the Ogumotori-goe section of the Nakahechi Route). After five kilometers you reach the stone mark, Cho-ishi, after which a steep descent, partially on a concrete road, brings you to a red bridge for crossing the Odomogawa River. The Cho-ishi is an old stone distance marker, where Cho indicates a distance of 109 meters. At this location you find the Cho-ishi indicating a distance to Hongu Taisha of around 66 kilometers. After the bridge the road goes up steep again until you reach a small village. At this village there is a resting point and another local black stamp.

After the Village you finally leave the road again, and walk on a relaxing forest trail. The trail goes up continuously, and there are some steep sections, but generally it is easy to walk.

After some 3 kilometers the forest trail ends, and you need to continue on a main road. It is road number 371, also called the Koya-Ryujin Skyline. There is little traffic on this road, so it is safe to walk in the gutter. Just be careful along the narrow bends in the road, where the drivers see you only last minute. You can, however, easily hear the cars approaching and make sure that you are at a safe place on the side of the road.

Call # 5: Along the way I came across a bear warning shield, which looked unofficial. This is the only bear warning I came across on the Nakahechi and Kohechi Routes, though there are small bears in the Kii Mountains, even if I did not encounter any bears. Tourist Information should provide better guidance on this risk.

At this point you are almost half way already. For about 2 kilometers the road snakes up, and you have some nice views on the surrounding mountains. At the Mitzu-ga-mine fork you leave the tarmac and continue on the forest trail, which takes you to the top of a hill through a steep path.

The climb is not long, and soon the trail changes to an asphalt road. It is a mountain road without any traffic. Apart from some short uphill walks, the route basically trails down till you reach Omata. The asphalt road is gently sloping down, so it is easy to walk for the next several kilometers, till you arrive at the Imanishi-tsuji junction. There you change back to the forest trail, a narrow path further sloping down, from where you regularly have a view on the asphalt road which follows the same direction. For about a kilometer you can enjoy the fresh scents of the pine trees and soft underfoot, till the trail continues on the same asphalt road again till the Taira-tsuji junction. Here you can see the stone izo of a Kumano Kodo pilgrim of the old ages. From there the descent to Omata becomes relatively steep. First through the forest, then a short section of the road, and again a very steep decline on the forest trail. When you step on the main road in Omata, you are almost immediately at the bus stop. Though don't get your hopes up for a regular bus service at this location: in season a bus comes twice a day, out of season there is no bus at all.

The best way to spend the night is to stay at one of the accommodations in Omata. There are three hotels in the area, of which the Nosegawa hotel is probably the largest. When you reach the bus stop and the bridge over the river, you might think that you are done. Well, you are when you have a tour-operator pick you up with a tour bus and escort you to a hotel in another location. The Nosegawa hotel is yet another 3.1 kilometers up the mountain road, basically in the same direction where you just came from, just a different road. The asphalt road has little traffic, but it continuously goes up, alongside a river. You will feel it in your calves when you finally arrive at the hotel 45 minutes later.

This hotel has a hot spring bath, so it is great to have your leg muscles relax in the 42-degree Celsius water. Do your stretching and you will be fit again for the next day. As a nice extra, the washing area at the hot spring offers a salt scrub, doing wonders for your skin. The room is tidy and clean, with tatami mats and a futon to sleep on, and has its own toilet and sink, unlike at the Shukubo in Koyasan. The bath is however shared, the typical hot spring bath.

To summarize the day: from Koyasan to the first pass at about 1'100 meters the trail is mostly on a concrete road, gently sloping up. After the pass you have some steep descents till you reach the bridge over the Odomogawa River, after which it goes up steeply again.

You walk about 65% of the time on concrete or asphalt roads, but there is little-to-no traffic. The last 40% of your hike only goes down, first gradually, towards the end more steeply. The day statistic above, indicating a trail length of 18.5 kilometers does not include the 3.1 kilometers that you need walk up the mountain again over an asphalt road to reach the Nosegawa hotel. That totals it to 21.6 kilometers.

This route gets a 3 out of 5 in the difficulty rating because most of the trail is on asphalt road and not so steep, and most of the altitude meters are made descending.

I did not encounter any other hikers that day, not in my direction, nor in the opposite direction. Other than me, the trail was deserted during the morning time of my hike.

Highlight of this part: Viewpoints on the mountain ranges and solitude of the route.

Low point of this part: about 65% of the route has concrete or asphalt road. At the end the additional 3.1 kilometers up the road to get to the hotel.

Call # 6: The Nakahechi Route has made its many stamps to be collected like a small treasure hunt. It could be interesting for the Kohechi Route to place more stamps along the path (not just at the beginning and end) to add a treasure hunt experience for the hiker.

Photos of the Section

Kohechi Trail Head

Steep road

Otaki-guchi Nyonin-do site memorial stamp

Easy Road climb

This car did not make it

Different Trail Signs

Wide views

Susuki-toge pass at ca. 1'100 meters

Steep descent on easy under footing

Easy forest trail

Solitude

Cho-ishi

Colors of the forest

Steep and slippery road descent

The red bridge in the valley

Odonogawa River

Steep road ascent

Resting place at Otaki Village

Non-official route stamp

Kumano Kodo

Forest trails

Along the Koya-Ryujin Skyline

Take the trail on the left, leaving the Skyline

Bear warning   *Sign post*

View

Trail

Deserted forest road

Panoramic views

Winding road and forest trail

Stone jizo along the trail

The road is never far away

Another Jizo for your protection and guidance

That's where you are going

Steep descent towards Omata

Kawaharari River in Omata

Don't wait for the bus

Ending point of the section: Omata bashi Bridge

Up the road again to Nosegawa Spa

Section 2: Omata to Miura-guchi

Key Data

Distance: ca. 16.2 km
Duration: ca. 4 to 6 hrs.
Altitude meters: ca. 2'040 meters
Lowest altitude: ca. 333 meters
Highest altitude: ca. 1'245 meters
Stamps at: Your hotel at Miura-guchi (39).
Difficulty: 5 out of 5
Percentage of road: ca. 5%

Section 2	Omata to Miura-guchi	1'250					1'250
		1'000					1'000
		750					750
		500					500
		250					250
		0					0

39

Description of the Section

In case you spent the night at the Nosegawa hotel, your day starts with 3.1 km (30 minutes) downhill on the road to get to the Omata bridge, before you can continue with the Kumano Kodo trail. These kilometers, time and also additional altitude meters need to be added to the above key data.

Cross the bridge and keep left on a small road going up extremely steep, with houses along the side for about 500 meters. At the end of the concrete road you pass a small cemetery and the path changes into a forest trail. The trail continues to go up the mountain with an extremely steep path, in a zig-sag direction till the 1.5 kilometer point. After that the trail continues to rise, at some points steep, at other stretches gentler, till you reach the first pass of the day, the Hinoki-toge pass at about 1'200 meters, ca. 3.7 kilometers after Omata. According to folktales, Kobo Daishi threw away his chopsticks at this pass, later growing into a cypress tree.

After that pass, the trail slopes down quite steeply, until it starts climbing again till you arrive at the Obato-toge pass at ca. 1'245 meters. This point is reached ca. 6.4 kilometers after the start and is considered as one of the top 200 mountains in Japan, offering panoramic views towards inner Koya, the Omine mountain Range as well as towards mount Goma-danzan. The hut at the pass level enables an overnight stay. For the remainder of the ca. 9.8 kilometers the path basically goes down, however not continuously. There are multiple sections along the remainder of the way which go up steeply and come down steeply again. Quite a section of the path is extremely narrow and has deep cliffs on the left side. It seems that along this part of the route there have been many earth and rock slides, which makes it rather dangerous to walk along certain ridges.

At the ruins of the Uenishi House (an old Inn and Teahouse) the trail takes a different route from a formerly used path. The old path is blocked. According to the map, there should be signposts guiding the way to the alternative path. However, there are no signposts, though the new path is guided by long ribbon hung up between the trees, and pink ribbons tied to trees at a certain distance.

Call # 7: There were only few signposts, and most of the signposts were in Japanese. There were a few normal Kumano Kodo signposts on critical junctions and locations, but those were not many. Better and more consistent signposting would help the hiker along the right path.

This detour starts with a steep climb up a hill, followed by a steep descent on the other side. After that it flattens a bit, but there is a continuous exchange of short up-hills and steep down-hills. Along a further part, the trail is narrow and passes along steep cliffs, making this a second dangerous section. Earth and rock slides have partially wiped away the path and several makeshift repairs have been made to improve safety. The trail continues with steep downhill descents, mostly through soft soil, but also a part where the trail is covered with flagstones. Unlike at the sections of the Nakahechi Route, these flagstones are dry. They are not slippery because they are free of moss, making them less dangerous to traverse. You can already hear the Kannogawa River, while the descent continues very steeply. The path descends steeply till you reach the Obako-dake trailhead, where you arrive at a local road number 733. You cross the red bridge and follow the road around several bends and a short tunnel till you arrive at Miura-guchi.

The time table at the bus stop shows that a bus passes through this village only three times a day. So unless you are part of a tour group and being picked up by a charter coach, you will either need the bus to get away from of this location, or you need a local hotel. Looking at the bus time table, it might be difficult to plan your arrival avoiding a long wait at the bus stop. And where does this bus lead to anyway? A location where there will be hotels available? Probably, but you are in the middle of the mountains, and there are only other small villages in the valleys, so it is better to stay at one of the three Minshuku in Miura-guchi. This will need to be booked in advance, and can be done via the Kumano Kodo Travel Community Reservation System.

Tip # 17: Book your stays along the Kohechi Route long in advance. This is easily done via the Kumano Travel Office (www.kumano-travel.com) Community Reservation System.

I am staying in Minshuku Mandokoro, and as all signs in the village are only in Japanese, I need to ask at a local house for directions. The friendly lady sends me back for about 800 meters up the road, close to the tunnel which I passed before. About some 100 meters before I arrive there, a little old lady is already waving at me and calling out in Japanese. Apparently the woman whom I asked for directions called ahead to let the owner of the Minshuku know that a foreign traveler was arriving.

A Minshuku is an accommodation where you don't have a private room, but where the sleeping space of tatami mats is separated by sliding doors in little rooms. In such a room you have only a futon, blanket and a basket with your towel and Yukata. The shower and toilet are shared between the visitors, together with the owners. Meals are taken in a separate room, by the visitors together. There is little privacy, as during day time most sliding doors are open.

Upon arrival, get your stamps first, as you might forget otherwise. One stamp in the special Kohechi booklet and one stamp in the general Kumano Kodo stamp booklet. As you can clearly see, the stamp represents the 500 years old cedar tree, which you will see right after the start of the next section, when leaving Miura-guchi. Unfortunately, there are no Onsen hot springs at this location, so a shower will have to do, followed by stretching the tired legs. The legs and particularly the knees have been heavily impacted by the long and steep descents for the last two and a half hours of the trek. The distance for today was little over 16 kilometers, but add to that the walk from the hotel in Omata, and to the Minshuku, and you come to more than 20 kilometers in a constant up-hill and down-hill strides.

Call # 8: Distance markers changed along the way. It started with small yellow stickers, disappeared for a while and then stone markers every once in a while. The Nara and Wakayama Prefectures should better coordinate consistency of the distance markers.

To summarize the day: from Omata the climb to the first pass is extremely steep and tough. After that pass you have some steep descents, followed by a long climb to the second and highest pass. From there it is a long descent with continuously going up-hill and down-hill, really very tiring. Parts of the path are very dangerous because of rock slides and cliffs on your left side, combined with a very narrow path. Basically the whole trail was in the forest, so that was very nice, although the April wind at the higher altitudes was still very cold.

This route gets a 5 out of 5 in the difficulty rating because of the high altitude meters covered in a relatively short distance and the fact that the two passes have very steep climbs.

I encountered only one elderly Japanese couple that was hiking the same route as I. Other than them, the trail was deserted and I did not meet any other people for more than three and a half hours during the morning time of my hike.

Tip # 18: You are hiking through remote and isolated mountain areas. During most of the Kohechi trail there is cellphone reception, so make sure that you carry a cellphone for emergency cases, particularly when you are travelling alone. Have the local emergency numbers pre-programmed.

There is only one resting point with a toilet, at the Obako-toge pass after almost six and a half kilometers. There are no service points, nor any places where you can get drinking water. So bring enough water and make sure that you have a packed lunch or other food with you. This route is all mountainous and forest.

Highlight of this part: Viewpoints on the mountain ranges and solitude of the route.

Low point of this part: Several dangerous sections along cliffs and rockslides. Cold April wind. Extremely long and steep descent, making it very hard on the knees. No hot spring bath in Miura-guchi.

Photos of the Section

From Nosegawa Spa to Omata Bashi Bridge

Through Omata Village

Along Jizo wearing bibs

Steep up, along a graveyard

Steep up following Japanese signs

Steep up

Panoramic view

Morning sun

Hinoki-toge pass at ca. 1'200 meters

Forest trails

Obako-toge pass at ca. 1'245 meters

Dangerous descents

Along the ridge

Detour from previous trail

Trail along landslides

Signposts

Shrine with Kobo Daishi statue

Beautiful forest trail

Kumano Kodo

Trail repairs

View

Steep descent

Jizo Statute

Uneven path

That's where you are going

The end of the previous trail

The end of the current trail

Mitadani-bashi Bridge

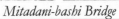

Hans Beumer

Through the tunnel to Miura-guchi Village

Miura-guchi bus stop

Kannogawa River

323

Minshuku Mandokoro

Section 3: Miura-guchi to Totsukawa

Key Data

Distance:	ca. 20.1 km
Duration:	ca. 5 to 7 hrs.
Altitude meters:	ca. 1'900 meters
Lowest altitude:	ca. 160 meters
Highest altitude:	ca. 1'080 meters
Stamps at:	Your hotel at Totsukawa (40).
Difficulty:	4 out of 5
Percentage of road:	ca. 38%

KOHECHI ROUTE			Distance					
(all road times are estimates based on personal experiences)		Altitude	0 km	5 km	10 km	15 km	20 km	Altitude
		1'250						1'250
		1'000						1'000
Section 3	Miura-guchi	750						750
	to Totsukawa	500						500
		250						250
		0						0

40

Description of the Section

In Miura-guchi you cross the Funato-bashi suspension foot bridge, and at the end turn left bringing you immediately on the trail, which passes some houses, till you enter the soft forest path. You pass rice terraces in a desolate state, as if they are not in use anymore. The ascent is steep, partially zig-sag up the mountain, but the path is easy to walk. The underfoot is of soft forest earth, with only very few passages consisting of rocks or steps.

You pass a number of enormous majestically twisted 500-year-old cedar trees, and a bit further up the path you come to a small natural spring, called Sanju-cho.

The last kilometers to the Miura-toge pass manifest the results of landslides and deforestation. You pass through a large area with cut down trees, where the soil is barely held together anymore. Because the trail cuts right through this area, authorities have put up blue mesh to guide the hiker and prevent the trail from disruption by earth/stone slides, providing a safe passage for the hiker. It is an extraordinary sight. At the pass level of 1'080 meters, there is a resting area, restroom and a large table with information. There are some dirt roads for the foresters at the top of the pass, so it is not your typical mountain trail pass, as it has been in the last days.

The trail continues straight ahead over the pass and keeps its soft underfoot. It is easy to descent on this path, though there are a couple of short areas where the trail becomes very narrow and has deep cliffs (some of them caused by landslides) on the left side of the path. The path mostly has the mountain on its right side, but which after some twists and turns also changes to the left side. When you depart early morning and are the first on the trail, you will walk into spider webs that hang between the trees over the path. You get them on your arms and in your face, and you often need to wipe the thin threads away.

About half way the descent the path follows a new trail; it separates from the old trail, which is blocked by landslides. This new trail first goes up quite steeply until you walk more or less flat on a ridge with forests and steep downslopes on the left as well as the right side of the trail. It is beautiful and the panoramic views on the other mountain ranges.

Further down you pass the Yagura-kannon-do on your left side, right after a turn. There are a few more stretches where the path narrows and goes dangerously close between rocks on your left side and steep abyss on your right side. At some of these stretches, ropes have been hung for safety of the hikers.

After some deserted houses you trail further down till you arrive at a small road. You follow the road to the left, downhill, until a sign shows you the path back into the forest to the right, further down the hill. This forest path is basically a shortcut from the road, which makes a longer loop to go down. You arrive at a lower section of the road, where there is only a Japanese signpost. Follow this road 50 meters to the left, going up the hill again, as it leads to the continuation of the forest path down the mountain. Then after little more than 11 kilometers you arrive at road nr. 425, where you turn left.

This road follows the Nishigawa River with its many bends till you arrive at Totsukawa. The road is easy to walk, with little traffic, though it still goes up-hill and down-hill. The views on the river are beautiful against the backset of the dark green mountain ranges. You pass several construction sites, where workers are trying to better control the power of the water by making fortifications. Don't take any of the side roads, keep following the 425 for almost 9 kilometers in total. The road passes through small villages where you are able to obtain drinks from vending machines. You will still need a lunch packet for the day.

I am in hotel Subaru, which is situated shortly before Totsukawa. It has a hot spring which does wonders for the strained leg muscles. Just be aware that the hot spring water coming from deep in the earth is accompanied by a sulfur smell, the smell of rotten eggs. The smell is strongest in the inside bath, while in the outside bath you hardly smell it. Totsukawa is famous for its Onsen or hot springs and there are many hotels and ryokans in the area. As evidenced by the list of hotels where you can get the stamp for this section of the Kohechi route, there are 10 listed. The list also shows that you can get your stamp at the Nara Kotsu Bus Center in Totsukawa, just in case you decide not to stay in a hotel at this location.

I did not encounter any other hikers today, not in my direction, nor in the opposite direction during the time that I was walking. Other than me, the trail was deserted, though in the Minshuku in Miura-guchi I did meet an elderly Japanese couple and an elderly single Japanese man hiking the route as well.

To summarize the day: It is a long walk, though not with maximum difficulty, despite the high number of altitude meters. The trek starts with a steep climb from ca. 333 meters to ca. 1'080 meters within ca. 4.3 kilometers, after which there is a long descent for ca. 7 kilometers. During this descent, you reduce your elevation from ca. 1'080 meters to ca. 223 meters, generally on gentle slopes, with only a few steep parts. The final ca. 8.8 kilometer is on the road, which goes a bit up-hill and down-hill, but finally descends for ca. 59 elevation meters. This section receives a 4 out of 5 on the scale of difficulty.

Highlight of this part: Viewpoints on the mountain ranges and solitude of the route. Easy forest underfoot on the trail. Views along the Nishigawa River from the road.
Low point of this part: The deforestation shortly before the Miura-toge pass. Ca. 38% of the route is on asphalt road.

Photos of the Section

Funato-bashi Bridge

Trail head

Steep climbs

Dry rice paddies

Steep stone slopes

Lose rocks under-foot

500 years old twisted Cedar tree

Sanju-cho Spring

Steep zig-sag up

Trail repaired after landslide

Detour because of landslides

Deforestation

Dangerous pathway

Shielded by blue mesh

Panoramic view

End of the detour

Miura-toge pass at ca. 1'080 meters

Makeshift signs

Makeshift bridges

Forest trail

Makeshift railing

Jizo

Steep descent

Spring colors

Ridge trail

Yagura Kannon-do

Kannon Statue

Don't slip to the right

Nearing road nr. 425

Go down the trail

50 meters to the left, up the road

Down the steps   *Through the forest to the road*

Keep following road nr. 425

Along the Nishigawa River

Past the local Shrine

In the direction of Totsukawa Spa

Along river construction works

Through Villages on road nr. 425

Past major river bed construction

Looking at beautiful mountain panoramas

As well as river views

The Onsen changing room at Hotel Subaru, Totsukawa

Washing area

Outside and inside hot spring bath

Section 4: Totsukawa to Hongu Taisha Grand Shrine

Key Data

Distance:	ca. 18.5 km
Duration:	ca. 5 to 7 hrs.
Altitude meters:	ca. 2'300 meters
Lowest altitude:	ca. 90 meters
Highest altitude:	ca. 1'060 meters,
Stamps at:	Hatenashi Settlement (41), Hongu Taisha Grand Shrine (18).
Difficulty:	5 out of 5
Percentage of road:	ca. 14%

		1'250						1'250
	Totsukawa to Hongu	1'000						1'000
Section 4	Taisha	750						750
	Grand	500						500
	Shrine	250						250
		0						0

The Kumano trail map for this Section is split in two parts. The first part covers the route from Totsukawa to Yakio Bus Station and includes the Hatenashi-toge pass at ca. 1'060 meters, with a trail distance of about 12 kilometers. It is this part which has the high number of altitude meters. The second part is from Yakio Bus Station to the Kumano Hongu Grand Shrine, and covers about 6.5 kilometers, with very limited altitude meters.

41   *18*

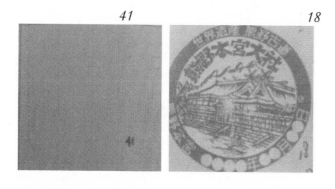

Description of the Section

On the day that I walk this section of the Kohechi Route, it is severely bad weather from my start at 7:30 a.m. till noon. There is extremely heavy rainfall accompanied by strong winds. Fortunately, it is not cold. The heavy rainfall already started during the night, so by the time that I get to the trail, the forest path is already soaked and little streams of water flow down the path. For the few stretches where the path is horizontal, large pools of water formed. I need to zig-sag the path for most of the way going up-hill and down-hill, in order to avoid the little streams and puddles of water, and find a foothold that is least wet. There are quite a few sections with stones and rocks, which have become extremely slippery. Within 15 minutes my hiking shoes and socks are soaked, as I do not wear waterproof shoes. It feels like the soles of my shoes have no grip anymore, and I slip many times during the descent. Fortunately, I can somehow keep my balance, and I do not fall. The heavy rainfall has a big impact on the hardship during the trekking, so under such conditions you may easily add 1 to 1.5 points on the difficulty rating. Trekking in the Kii Mountains with such high altitude meters to be covered made this my most difficult day of the Kohechi Route. On this section 4 of the Kohechi Route, there were no real dry resting places for the first ca. 14 kilometers. Heavy rainfall and strong winds are however very common in the Kii Mountains. Whenever you plan your hiking and pilgrimage, you are bound to have one or multiple days of rain. So come prepared.

Tip # 19: Come prepared with rain gear. In case you have flexibility in your day planning you could also sit out a half day or day of rain.

When leaving the Subaru hotel, turn right, through a small tunnel, not the road tunnel on the left side of the hotel. The small tunnel gets you to a hanging foot bridge over the Kamiyunokawa River. When I crossed the foot bridge, it was being whipped by rain and wind and shaking dangerously. I made it across safely, but about halfway it was swinging so much from the wind and my pace movement, that I had to pause until the swinging was reduced.

At the other side of the river bank, the path goes immediately into the forest and goes up steeply with zig-sag directions on flagstones. After ca.

1.5 kilometers you arrive at the Hatenashi Village where you walk between some houses. It is at this location where you need to get your first stamp for the day. There is, however, no box or little wooden house on a pole to be seen with a stamp. I looked at all the places along the path and even knocked on the door of one of the houses in order to ask for the location of the stamp. But nobody came to the door, so I continued on the trail, without the stamp.

When I was at the Tourist Information Center in Hongu Taisha later that afternoon, I told them about my missing stamp. The friendly manager told me that this was a common problem as this stamp is being stored at one of the private houses in the Village. Apparently the Japanese stamp booklet identifies, in Japanese, at which house this stamp can be obtained. The night before I had actually asked about this at the Subaru hotel, but they did not know the exact location either. So how should a foreign pilgrim know about this? This should really be changed, and this stamp should be made available for easy public access without the involvement of and dependence on a private person.

Call # 5: The stamp at the Hatenashi Settlement is at a private house. Access to this stamp should be made easier and public, independent from a private person. At least the stamp should be left outside for easy access during any time of the day.

After the village, the path continues in the forest with mostly steep upslope tracks, some with steps, some with stones, some with forest under footing. When getting higher, there are several nice viewpoints. Though because of the bad weather and low overhanging clouds, the panoramic views are not so clear.

Along the way you pass a flat and open area called 'Rain-fed rice paddies remains'. Growing rice requires large quantities of water, and the fact that locals were able to grow rice based on the regular rainfall shows how wet it can be in the Kii Mountains.

One thing is special about the route from Totsukawa to Yakio: it has 33 small stone Kannon statues along the path. A Kannon is a Buddhist figure and an icon in Japanese culture, being represented in many temples as one of the most important deities. A deity is a being that is thought of as holy and sacred. The little stone statues represent the Kannon Bodhisattva, the great savior to those suffering. Because the Kumano Kodo trail starts from the hanging bridge in Totsukawa, and not from the Ichizako Bus Stop, you will miss the three Kannon numbered 33, 32 and 31. At the Hatenashi Village you will see your first Kannon numbered 30. Then along the whole trail they are spread out in regular distances, till you see the last one with number 1 close to the Yakio Bus Stop. The statues along this route were erected around the year 1923.

Shortly before the pass, you pass the Hatenashi Kannon-do temple, containing three stone statues. It includes the eleven-faced Kannon, which represents the ten sacred vows of Buddha to safeguard Beings from suffering. At the pass level, there are sign posts and the 17th Kannon statue but nothing more. There is no shelter to sit in a dry place. It storms at the pass level, and instead of taking a rest, a drink and a bite, I have to push on. The wind is whipping the rain too hard to take off my backpack cover and open the bag.

Call # 16: There is no shelter at the Hatenashi-toge pass, like at most other passes. A shelter would be convenient to rest. In the bad weather during my passing, I had no choice but to continue and complete the descent till I got to the Michi-no-eki rest stop, which was ca. 7 kilometers after the top.

The descent is steep for most of the way. It is extremely slippery on the stones. At this side of the mountain it is raining less, but instead the wind is much stronger, whipping the drops from the leaves of the trees. There are less puddles and fewer water streams down the path, but because of the wetness of the rocks and my shoes, I still need to place my feet with caution. Both the ascent as well as the descent are slow. Much slower than my normal speed. There are a couple of stretches where the trail is dangerously narrow and along a steep cliff. At some of these locations ropes have been attached on the rock walls. The descent ends on the street number 168 in Yakio, close to the bus stop.

When arriving on the road nr. 168, take a right over the bridge and keep following the horizontal pedestrian path along the road and the Kumanogawa River till you reach the Michi-no-eki store, information center and resting place after ca. 1.3 kilometers. The Kumano Kodo path continues to the right of the large parking place, along the road. Walk on the asphalt road and continue to follow road nr. 168 until a small road leads off to the right after little less than a kilometer. There is a big signpost on the 168 road, so you can't miss it. This little road has no traffic and goes uphill for a short while till you get to the Sangen-jaya site, where the trail converges with the final 2 kilometers of the Nakahechi Route, section 2 Tsugizakura-oji to Hongu Taisha.

Shortly before the Sangen-jaya site, you come across sign with a snake warning and indeed a snake crosses my path just a meter in front of me. They warn for vipers, so it is good to carry a walking cane or hiking sticks.

Tip # 26: Carry a walking cane or hiking sticks, not only for providing support during ascents and descents, but also to fend off any snakes or other animals on the pathway.

The last kilometers have a beautiful path through a beautiful forest, right out of a Kumano Kodo brochure. The forest smells fresh after the morning rain, while the sun shines through the high trees. Despite the many stone steps it is relatively easy to walk and it is not steep in ascent or descent. Approximately a kilometer before Hongu Taisha you come across a sign that suggests a small detour to a view point. It is worthwhile to follow that path of that detour because it is relatively short and the view is really magnificent. Sure, a climb and a descent are involved, as usual along any of the trails, but it is worthwhile to do so. You have a panoramic view on the Kumano-gawa River and the Oyunohara giant gateway in the distance. Until 1889, the Kumano Hongu Taisha Grand Shrine was located at the location of this gateway. In those days it was on a sand bank in the middle of the river, whereas nowadays the Grand Shrine is on higher ground, safe from river flooding.

The final part of the trail climbs to ca. 213 meters in altitude before it descends to ca. 90 meters at the Grand Shrine of Hongu Taisha, where you arrive at the back entrance.

My hotel is not in Hongu Taisha but in Yunomine Onsen, hotel Ryokan Adumaya. So in this case, I continue my hike from Hongu Taisha to Yunomine Onsen, which adds another ca. 4.2 kilometers to my day, totaling it to ca. 22.7 kilometers. The extra hiking kilometers (which could also be done by bus) are really worthwhile, as this hotel has a hot spring bath, where it is great to relax your leg muscles in the 42 degrees' Celsius water. My room is tidy and clean, with tatami mats and a futon to sleep on. My room has its own toilet and sink, but the bath is shared, the typical hot spring bath. Dinner and breakfast are served in my room. My shoes were totally soaked from the rain of the whole morning, and the friendly lady at the front desk ensures me that my shoes will be dry again in the morning, putting a de-humidifier in each shoe. Internet is only available in the lobby.

This route gets a 5 out of 5 in the difficulty rating because of the high number of altitude meters of more than 2'300. It is the highest of the Kohechi route. In Totsukawa the trail starts immediately with an ascent of almost 900 altitude meters in ca. 6 kilometers, of which most is relatively steep. After the pass at ca. 1'060 meters it goes down immediately and relatively steep for most of the descent, taking ca. 6 kilometers to descend more than 950 altitude meters. After a stretch of flat road, the trail goes up again by ca. 120 altitude meters, after which it descends to Hongu Taisha by another ca. 132 altitude meters. This latter path starts out with a road, but soon changes into a trail with many stone steps.

I did not encounter any other hikers on this route, neither in my direction, nor in the opposite direction. Other than me, the trail was deserted till the Hongu Taisha Grand Shrine. It was probably due the extremely bad weather conditions of the morning, in combination with the less frequently traversed Kohechi Route. Shortly before the Grand Shrine there are usually quite a few people walking the ancient path.

Highlight of this part: Viewpoints along the way and solitude of the route. Relatively easy forest underfoot during most of the trail going up-hill and down-hill the Hatenashi-toge pass. Beautiful path and forest the last few kilometers before the Hongu Taisha Grand Shrine. The smell of the forest after the rain.

Low point of this part: The very high number of altitude meters. Steep ascents and descents in extreme weather conditions.

Photos of the Section

Foot bridge in heavy rain and storm

Steep up

Hatenashi Village *Rain fed rice paddies remains*

Stream down the trail *Kannon*

Kannon-do

Hatenashi-toge pass at 1'060 meters

Kannon along the way

Steep descents

Obscured view

Slippery and uneven

In the clouds

Keep descending   *To end of trail*

Follow the road and cross the bridge

Michi-no-eki

Keep left   *Stay on the road*

Take the road to the right

Follow the road up

Forest trail till you arrive at the intersection with the Nakahechi Route

Trail through beautiful environment

Still up and down, but easy to do

Final descent to Hongu Taisha

Hongu Taisha Shrine

Entrance to the main Shrine

The main Shrine

Main entrance gate

Hans Beumer

10 CALLS TO ACTION FOR LOCAL TOURIST OFFICES

During my two weeks stay in the Kii Mountains and my hiking along the Kumano Kodo trails, I came across a number of situations which have the potential to be improved. Addressing these situations will improve the experience and safety of the pilgrim who walks the Kumano Kodo Routes.

Below is the summary of the 10 'Calls to Action' that have been identified during my pilgrimage. Not surprisingly, 8 out of the 10 'Calls to Action' relate to the Kohechi Route.

The Nakahechi Route has a lot of (commercial and non-commercial) stakeholders, resulting in a high focus from Prefecture Authorities, local Tourist Offices and commercial businesses (such as accommodations and tour operators), which ensures that the tourists and visitors experiences are optimized.

This is quite different for the Kohechi Route. Koyasan, the starting point of the Kohechi Route, receives a similar high focus from Prefecture Authorities, local Tourist Offices and commercial businesses, but as soon as you set foot on the 70 kilometers of hiking trails, it is completely different. The trails lead you through isolated mountain ranges where only few pilgrims walk the pathways, and thus commercial interests are a lot lower. Still, I would like to call the Prefecture Authorities and local Tourist Offices into action to improve a number of requirements. It is a special experience to undergo the hardship, suffering and isolation during the Kohechi Route, and in itself this should not be changed. Compared to most parts of the Nakahechi Route, the Kohechi Route probably comes a lot closer to the suffering and hardship which the pilgrim had to endure a thousand years ago.

Kumano Kodo

I call on the relevant Prefecture Authorities and local Tourist Offices to address the following topics:
Chapter 2

Cali # 1: There are six Kumano Kodo Routes, but only three of them have route maps and trail details in the English language. For the Sections 6 and 7 of the Nakahechi Route, only Japanese language trails maps are available as well. The Tourist Offices of the related Prefectures should consider making these route maps available in English as well.

Chapter 6, section 5

Cali # 2: The Tourist Information Center in Hongu Taisha should make sure that stamp nr. 34 is well visible and permanently obtainable at the Kamikura-jinja Shrine.

Cali # 3: The sequence of the stamps between the River Boat Tour center (nr. 36) and Ukegawa (nr. 21) should be reversed in the Kumano Kodo Stamp list to adjust to the historically correct sequence of the pilgrimage route.

Chapter 7, section 1

Cali # 4: The local black stamp seems to be created by the local village. It would be better to have all stamps along the route coordinated with the Koyasan Tourist Office and made part of the official Kumano Kodo stamps.

Cali # 5: Along the way I came across a bear warning shield, which looked unofficial. This is the only bear warning I came across on the Nakahechi and Kohechi Routes, though there are small bears in the Kii Mountains, even if I did not encounter any bears. Tourist Information should provide better guidance on this risk.

Cali # 6: The Nakahechi Route has made its many stamps to be collected like a small treasure hunt. It could be interesting for the Kohechi Route to place more stamps along the path (not just at the beginning and end) to add a treasure hunt experience for the hiker.

368

Chapter 7, section 2

Call # 7: There were only few signposts, and most of the signposts were in Japanese. There were a few normal Kumano Kodo signposts on critical junctions and locations, but those were not many. Better and more consistent signposting would help the hiker along the right path.

Call # 8: Distance markers changed along the way. It started with small yellow stickers, disappeared for a while and then stone markers every once in a while. The Nara and Wakayama Prefectures should better coordinate consistency of the distance markers.

Chapter 7, section 4

Call # 9: The stamp at the Hatenashi Settlement is at a private house. Access to this stamp should be made easier and public, independent from a private person. At least the stamp should be left outside for easy access during any time of the day.

Call # 10: There is no shelter at the Hatenashi-toge pass, like at most other passes. A shelter would be convenient to rest. In the bad weather during my passing, I had no choice but to continue and complete the descent till I got to the Michi-no-eki rest stop, which was ca. 7 kilometers after the top.

Kumano Kodo

BIBLIOGRAPHY

This travel guide presents the status of the Nakahechi and Kohechi Kumano Kodo pilgrimage trails as observed and experienced by the Author in April 2016. Due to local influences along these two pilgrimage routes, the future experiences may deviate from the Author's experiences. Although the Author has been diligent in putting together all information, he does not guarantee the complete accuracy of all information in this book. Your own experiences may deviate from the Author's experiences, and therefore this book should only be used as a guide for you to understand the Kumano Kodo, its challenges and rewards, as well as the ease or difficulties with which the local routes can be walked. Distances, durations and altitudes as described in the book are as accurate as possible, mostly concurring with the local route maps. However, there are certain measurement deviations from the local route maps, where the author has maintained his own measurements.

The majority of the information in this book, such as the detailed descriptions of the hiking sections, the experiences along the trails, the local cultural and travel experiences, are all based on the personal experience of the Author.

Information relating to historical and cultural facts of the Kumano Kodo, the Shrines, Temples, Kannon, Jizo, Oji, Teahouse remains, etc. comes from a number of external sources. The Author does not guarantee the historical and cultural accuracy and completeness of this kind of information provided by these external sources:

Dual Pilgrim, *www.spiritual-pilgrimages.com*, *2016*

Hongu Taisha Heritage Center, Verbal information provided by the staff at the Tourist Information Center, 2016

Kumanogawa River Boat Tour Center, *Brochure: Kumano River Boat Tour*, Shingu: Kumanogawa River Boat Tour Center, 2016

Kumanogawa River Boat Tour Center, Verbal information provided by the Tour Guide during the River Boat Tour and the Tour at Nachi Taisha, 2016

Tanabe City, Information tables along the trails, containing historical facts about landmarks along the Nakahechi Trails, 2016

Tanabe City Board of Education, Information tables along the trails containing historical facts about landmarks along the Nakahechi Trails, 2016

Tanabe City Kumano Tourism Bureau, *www.kumano-travel.com*, 2016

Tanabe City Kumano Tourism Bureau, *www.tb-kumano.jp*, 2016

Tanabe City Kumano Tourism Bureau and www.tb-kumano.jp, *Kumano Kodo Pilgrimage Route Maps (Nakahechi Routes)*, Tanabe: Tanabe City Kumano Tourism Bureau, 2015

Tanabe City Kumano Tourism Bureau, Tourist Center at Kii Tanabe Station, 2016

Totsukawa Board of Education, Information tables along the trails containing historical facts about landmarks along the Kohechi Trails, 2016

Totsukawa Village Tourism Promotion Division and www.vill.totsukawa.lg.jp, *Kumano Sankeimichi Kohechi, Walking the World Heritage (Kohechi Routes)*, Totsukawa: Totsukawa Village Tourism Promotion Division, 2012

UNESCO, *The World's Heritage, The definitive guide to all 1007 World heritage sites*, Paris: HarperCollins Publishers, 2015

Wakayama Prefecture, Information tables along the trails, containing historical facts about landmarks along the Nakahechi Trails and Koyasan, 2016

Wakayama Tourism Bureau, *Brochure: Guide to Koyasan,* Wakayama: Wakayama Tourism Bureau, 2016

Wakayama Tourism Bureau, *Brochure: Wakayama Sightseeing Guide, The Heart of the Japanese Soul,* Wakayama: Wakayama Tourism Bureau, 2016

Wakayama Tourism Bureau, *Brochure: World Heritage, Sacred Sites and Pilgrimage Routes in the Kii Mountain Range,* Wakayama: Wakayama Tourism Bureau, 2016

Kumano Kodo

ABOUT THE AUTHOR

drs. Hans Beumer is an enthusiastic and seasoned traveler and a passionate Author. He has travelled all over the world for business and leisure, exploring many different cultures.

Throughout his lifetime, Hans has had an energetic drive to accomplish his goals. His personal vision is to make sure that his own goals generate a high added value contribution to the lives of other people. He sees it as the purpose of his life to help other people advance with their life. Privately he engages in philanthropy and supports the under-privileged children in India to help them advance to a meaningful life through education and a healthy and secure learning environment.

As an Author he shares his experiences with the world. His books are the carrying vehicles of his passion, and their publishing enables them to reach and touch the lives of many millions of other people on all continents. It is his aim to increase the level of happiness in the world and help to improve the lives of millions of other people.

The Author made his pilgrimage on the Kumano Kodo during a period of 14 days in April 2016.

Contact information: Please visit www.hansbeumer.com

Made in the USA
San Bernardino, CA
28 November 2017